Not a Man, and Yet a Man

Not a Man, and Yet a Man

A.A. Whitman

MINT EDITIONS

Not a Man, and Yet a Man was first published in 1877.

This edition published by Mint Editions 2021.

ISBN 9781513282619 | E-ISBN 9781513287638

Published by Mint Editions®

 MINT
EDITIONS

minteditionbooks.com

Publishing Director: Jennifer Newens
Design & Production: Rachel Lopez Metzger
Project Manager: Micaela Clark
Typesetting: Westchester Publishing Services

DEDICATION

To Those Who Loved the Negro in Mankind,
and Pitied Him,
And Stooped to Help Him in His Low Estate,
Assailed by Fierce Opinions,
And Told His Grievances in the Ear of God,
Until He Heard Them,
And Shook Proud Slavery on His Lap of Storm,
And Shook the Fetters From the Bondman's Heart.
To Those,
Who Safe Now in the Citadel of Right,
Their Conquests Hearing on the Tongue of Time,
Their Triumphs Reading in Young Freedom's Eyes,
And Looking Forward,
The Full Fruition of Their Bright Hopes See,
The Nations of All Earth Forever Free.
To Those,
The Abolition Fathers—
This Book is Inscribed
by the

—Author

Contents

Preface 9

Prologue 13

The Movers 17

Saville 19

The Old Sac Village 32

Pashepaho's Speech to the Young Men 38

Nanawawa's Suitors 41

Nanawawa's Lakelet 47

Death of Pashepaho 50

Saville in Trouble 52

The Fair Captive 68

Fort Dearborn 79

In the House of the Aylors 89

Flight of Leeona 118

The Runaway 132

Sussex Vale, Canada 145

The Little Green Cottage 147

One Snowy Night 151

The End of the Whole Matter 153

MISCELLANEOUS POEMS

PEACE 165

HYMN TO THE NATION 167

THE LUTE OF AFRIC'S TRIBE 170

TO THE STUDENT 172

CUSTAR'S LAST RIDE 174

SONNET.—THE MONTENEGRIN 176

SOLON STILES. HUMOROUS 177

THE THUNDER STORM 181

TO BABY'S CANARY, ACCIDENTALLY KILLED 182

THE DESERTED ROAD 183

OLD ABE, THE WAR EAGLE OF WISCONSIN 185

PROSPERITY AND ADVERSITY 186

A DREAM OF GLORY 187

MORTON 188

YE BARDS OF ENGLAND 195

THE GREAT STRIKE 197

THE TRAMP'S SOLILOQUY 199

A HINT 200

Preface

I was born in the Green River Country, Hart County, Kentucky, May 30th, 1851. I was a slave until the Emancipation. My parents left me and went to the Good Land when I was yet a boy. My chances for an education have not been good. In that matter, however, I have done what I could. I have labored with my hands, taught school, and preached a RISEN, present Savior—not a bad lot after all. I am now an Elder in the African Methodist Episcopal Church, the stationed pastor at Springfield, Ohio, and General Financial Agent of Wilberforce University. With this brief account of myself, I pass to notice the Institution in whose interest I have written, and whose permanent endowment I hope to secure.

Wilberforce University is situated three and one-half miles North-East of Xenia, Greene County, Ohio; surrounded by beautiful farms, and from the West, looked down upon by a group of heavily wooded hills. It is one of the most desirable College sites in Ohio. The locality is eminently healthy. A considerable creek, winding around the grounds to the Southward, drains the neighboring fields, and gives the whole surrounding an admirably neat aspect. A number of fine springs break out in the deep ravines around the College, bubbling and laughing, with lucid health sparkling in their faces. The campus is laid out on a beautiful plateau, lying South-East of the University, and covered by a splendid grove with here and there a neat cottage among the trees.

The Building

THE UNIVERSITY BUILDING IS OF substantial brick and slate roofed. The rooms are large and airy. The accommodations good. Probable value of buildings and grounds, (52 acres), sixty-five thousand dollars ($65,000.00). No incumbrances.

Mission

THE SCHOOL, THOUGH UNDER THE auspices of the A. M. E. Church, is STRICTLY NON-SECTARIAN in its pretensions, and has, as its general mission, the imparting of CHRISTIAN EDUCATION to the colored race. The special mission of the Normal and Scientific Departments is the preparation of Christian Teachers for Southern fields of labor. The Theological Department has, as its special work, the training of efficient preachers, to carry an enlightened Gospel among the freedmen.

The great and good founder of the institution, Bishop D. A. Payne, D. D., has lived to see much of the fruits of his labor in the last-named department. Bishop Payne came to the Presidency of the University when in its trembling infancy, and for fifteen years holding up the motto, "LIKE PRIEST, LIKE PEOPLE," he cried in the ears of the churches: "Give us educated preachers for the freedmen," until many big hearted and good young men rose up and followed him. His successor, the Rev. Benjamin F. Lee, B. D., one of his students, shows that he lacks nothing of his master's spirit, efficient in training, strong in intellect, replete in goodness and supported by a Faculty who share his rare qualities; he goes right to work with a VIM that means inspiration.

The Object of this Publication

MY OBJECT IN PLACING THESE verses before an intelligent people is, First, to carry to their minds the purpose of the founders of Wilberforce. That purpose, as stated in the last Catalogue of the Institution, is "An aim to inspire and increase in the pupil self-respect, self-control and self-development."

Now may I not hope that, however imperfect or faulty these lines may be, they will, in some measure show "self-development." And this is the very thing most needed among the poor colored young men of our country; and hence, an EMPHASIS of the claims of Wilberforce upon those who are interested in the welfare of the freedman. Very few of the colored students of our land, there are, who can depend upon their parents for efficient aid in going to school. Too many, alas, like the author, have No parents, No aid. How wise then the encouragement of an educational system of "self-development." With the motto, "ECONOMY, THRIFT, MANHOOD," the humble, poor young man, finds his way out of obscurity into usefulness.

The founders of Wilberforce, knowing best the needs of the classes among which she was destined to operate, knew best how to supply them; and in this arrangement they have been happy. The poor young man, without preparatory training, coming to Wilberforce, soon learns to study out problems for himself, and hence, to THINK for himself. He learns that if he cannot excel, he CAN do something else—he can do WHAT he can—he can try—he can dare to fail. He soon learns the difference between a successful DO-NOTHING, and an honorable failure. If such a young man leaves Wilberforce between terms, to gather means for his support, MARK YOU, he will return, and not only that, he will bring up his studies with him.

The production of NOT A MAN, AND YET A MAN, whatever it is, is owing to that spirit of "self-development" which Wilberforce inspires.

Secondly, my object in publishing is, to introduce myself to the people. Those who read will feel acquainted with me. Some may think well of me, and even INVITE me to talk with them about our Wilberforce. There is nothing like being kindly thought of by a people before you go among them. Certainly none will despise the effort.

And now, dear public, NOT A MAN, AND YET A MAN, comes to your doors, let him in! As to his merits, let readers judge.

Our canvassers get ONLY such part of the sales as will help them honestly to live. Purchase, therefore, remembering that your mite goes to the aid of a noble cause, and, if any one, after having read, feel to give of his earthly goods more largely, let him send such donations to the author at Springfield, Ohio.

Letters of comment on the merits of this work, and also of encouragement for Wilberforce, are SINCERELY solicited of the reader, by

THE AUTHOR

Prologue

The shepherd-king of Judah's olden days,
Waked his sweet harp to sing Jehovah's praise,
Then this his theme was in his happy hour:
"Captivity hath lost her horn of power.
The mighty Arm hath broke oppression's staff,
And drives the spoiler's hosts, as wind drives chaff,
And moves his kingdoms as the thistle down,
By wanton whirlwinds here and there is blown!"

How panting thousands of his faithful tribe,
Drank this sweet strain, no mortal can describe.
Young freedom then first raised his voice sublime,
And spoke his triumphs in the ear of Time.
The soldier sang it on his tented hill,
The maiden at her toilsome slow hand-mill;
The shepherd piped it where he sauntered 'mong
His bleating folds, and desert paths along;
And morn and eventide, the Temple's choir
Poured forth the strain, by matron joined and sire.
The wilderness and solitary waste,
With gladsome music woke, and joyous haste;
Engedi's palmy hills their voices gave,
And echo answered from the prophet's cave;—
"Ye seed of Jacob sound the jubilee,
The Lord hath triumphed and His hosts are free.
Spread thro' the heathen's land the joyous news,
The Mighty God's the refuge of the Jews!
Our shield and strength, our everlasting Sun,
And who shall gainsay what His hand hath done?"
Their sister nations heard the swelling strain,
And ages answered ages back again,
Till yet along the march of centuries
The idea of God and Freedom flies.
Sweet strain! How rapture in it yet is heard
Wherever righteousness her horn hath reared!
Remoteness lends a sweetness to the sound

By changes undisturbed, by lore not bound.
It lives while empires sink and pass away,
Wisdoms go out, and languages decay.

High o'er the heights of tall ambitions gaze,
Beyond proud emulation's wildest maze,
And Freedom there hath set her glorious stars,
Eternal more than Jupiter or Mars.
Her Washington rides first upon our sky,
Lending his brilliance to the thousands nigh.
Next Lincoln, whom a grateful nation mourns,
Shoots blazing from the age which he adorns.
Sinks on the eve of dreadful war's alarms,
But sinks with a saved nation in his arms!
And Old John Brown of Harper's Ferry fame,
Peace to his shade, and honor to his name,
The negro's light of hope, the friend of right,
Looms on life's deep, a melancholy light;
The comet of his age, ominous, lone,
And saddest that on earth has ever shone.
But peerless champion of Equal Rights,
Great Sumner STANDS, like those majestic hights
That guard New England shores from Ocean's shocks,
With lifted arms of everlasting rocks;
And with the strength of ages in their locks.
'Twas he who, on his bosom, bore a race,
And met their proud oppressor face to face;
Rose like some Ajax, in his ponderous strength,
And drove his lance, with all its trenchant length,
Full on the brazen disk of slav'ry's shield,
Until the monster wrong, beneath it reeled.
And when the smoke of war had cleared away,
And in the nation's sky there broke new day;
'Twas he, who, mailed in all the might of lore,
The valiant friends of mankind went before,
To wipe the blots of caste from freedom's code,
And all its axioms of wrong explode;
Lift equal justice up, exalt her laws,
And in her temple plead the black man's cause.

Let love lorn bards illuminate their lays,
With moonlight soft, and sing some Juno's praise;
Or whine with cadence sweet, and sickly sweet,
Their few torn hopes at some Diana's feet;
Let school-house heroes rave around the walls,
Where patriotism rises, treason falls,
Sing loud heroics of a glorious strand,
A freedom's eagle, and a white man's land;
Let fools pass by and wag their empty heads,
Deride the sons of Slavery's humble sheds,
And statesmen prate of law and precedence,
My pen appeals to right and common sense.
The black man has a cause, deny who dares,
And him to vindicate my muse prepares.
A part of this great nation's hist'ry, he
Has made in valor and fidelity.
His sweat has poured to swell our ample stores,
His blood run freely to defend our shores;
And prayers ascended to the Lord of all,
To save the nation from a direful fall.

Who has not felt in childhood's heart the thrill
Of bloody Georgetown and of Bunker's Hill?
Who has not heard the drums of freedom swell,
When Putnam triumphed and when Warren fell?
Proud were our sires, Ticonderoga's boast,
Fearless defenders of Atlantic's coast.
When from fair freedom's terraced hights, we turn
A backward gaze, our grateful bosoms burn,
To see those heroes with red battle clenched,
Till in brave blood their humble fields are drenched.
With Valley Forge's snowy locks to see
The desp'rate fingers of young liberty,
Grappling, and see his valiant misery;
And then o'er Delaware's rough wint'ry stream,
To see a thousand loyal muskets gleam
In night's cold face; and hear the strong brave oars
That meet the hurrying ice between the shores!

And can we then forget that patriots, black,
Marched with white brothers to the dread attack?

And when in these late years, the war fiend came,
On tempest horsed, and waved a sword of flame,
When giant treason shook his locks of gore,
And from the East to West the Union tore;
When our free institutions shook and reeled,
Hope turned her eyes towards the battle-field;
And loyal hearts that ne'er before had quaked,
Then quaked, and all their hoarded riches staked.
A nation's hands were then imploring raised,
While freedom's arch with bolts of ruin blazed.
Where then the prowess of a century,
The loud boast of white-handed chivalry?
Where, when in triumph wild, the Southern hordes
Unbent their strength, and drew their fearless swords?
Ah! well, we prayed, and God in his own time,
His sable answer sent on Dixie's clime.
The strong armed negro threw off slavery's yoke,
And loud as thunder on the world's ear broke
His shouts of ONWARD! To the front he went,
And in the smoke and din of battle blent,
With brothers white, where color nothing meant.
And there, till our victorious banner swept
Once more the hights of freedom, and we wept
For joy, he stood beneath our starlit dome,
Until a grateful UNION called him home.

Now let the nation fling him from her arms,
Forget the part he bore, when war's alarms
Were rumbling hoarsely in her troubled ear,
And direful overthrow was plainly near;
Forget the hands that caught her falling stars,
And tore loud triumph from the flaunting bars
Of treason; yea, despise the sable race,
And music then will breathe the name with praise!

The Movers

'Twas in the long ago,
'Twas in the age of woods
Of Young America,
That moving, rattling, slow
Towards the Western plain,
A single settler's train,
Drawn on by oxen teams,
Was seen, as when in dreams,
Strange sights and solitudes,
Upon our vision play.

The tall forests swim in a crimson sea,
Out of whose bright depths rising silently,
Great golden spires shoot into the skies,
Among the isles of cloud-land high, that rise,
Float, scatter, burst, drift off, and slowly fade,
Deep in the twilight, shade succeeding shade.
And by yon leaning rocks beneath the hill
Whose sloping base, a peaceful streamlet laves,
With fitful joyance bubbling in its waves,
The train guard pausing, winds his signal shrill.
Long roll the echoes, and the patient train,
In order halt along the silent plain.
From under wagon covers eight or nine,
Two anxious rows of female faces shine,
And whispers buzz from lips to lips around:
"That's Rodney's horn!" "Is this the camping ground?"
Loud low the oxen, leaning in their gear,
Replying heifers low along the rear;
And ere the seated driver drops his threads,
Come leaping on and toss their hornless heads.
Mark how enjoyment this wild scene pervades,
How ruddy maidens vie with ruddy maids;
These gathering fagots from yon lofty wood;
They ranging vessels and preparing food;

While seated round, their lordly umpires rest
On upturned stones, and view them doubly blest,

Such were the scenes the early travelers met,
When they towards the West their faces set.
Then, movers all their earthly ware would load,
And drive a whole great farm of stock upon the road.
Moving was moving then. The house cat e'en,
High in her sleepy reign was onward seen,
Riding, among utensils old and rare,
And roost and all, the ancient cock was there;
And thro' the silent forest blew his horn,
By day occasional, but always night and morn.

SAVILLE

Fair Saville! earliest village of the wood,
To break the reign of ancient solitude,
Where erst the dusky tennants of the shade,
Along the Mississippi's waters strayed;
Thou once did flourish on the lap of fame,
When to thy rude abodes adventure's wand'ring footsteps came.

I turn with reverential step and slow,
To trace the scenes my recollections know.
Where now thy cliffs bleak winter's wiles oppose,
When through the screeching air his blasts he throws,
There warring totems once prolonged their stay,
And then e'en with reluctance went their way.
And where yon blossomed fields, and orchards green,
Fresh meadows, and contented flocks are seen,
There erst the Indian reared his wigwam rude,
Deep in the wide forest's pathless solitude.

Dear to me yet, and every day more dear,
Familiar sounds revive upon my ear;
Familiar scenes come to me o'er the past,
And I, recoiling from the Future vast,
Revisit in my dreams and solitude,
The pleasant places of thy borders rude.
Thus, when from tempest-brooding heav'ns I fly;
When life's meridian's in a pensive sky,
Back to the charms of other days I come,
And seem a traveler returning home.

Then cumbrous backwoods life wide o'er the vale,
Heard a responsive tongue in every gale.
Loud baying hounds pressed hard the fleety deer,
Replying horns pursued along the rear,
Wild song attuned the breezy throat of morn;
The plowman whistled to his growing corn,
And lads with hoes, garrulous as they went,

Close on his heels their nimble footsteps bent.
And there was heard from morn till evening late
The various accents of a happy state,
The waste echoing to the axe remote,
The anvil groaning as the blacksmith smote,
The plashy labors of the slumb'rous mill,
The brook reposing as the wheel stood still;
Loud shouts arising childhood's sports among,
And matrons scolding as their flax wheels sung.

And often gathered when the joyous Spring,
Had livened Winter's latest lingering,
When all the voiceless wastes of recent gloom
Awoke to song and warbled into bloom;
Beneath the spreading shades that arch yon green
In happy groups the village train were seen.
Near where yon footpath climbs behind the town,
And straggles off into a hazel down,
Their wonted sports through shining hours would stray,
Till time unnoticed brought the close of day;
And silent wheeling, scarce above the fence,
The crooked bat did aimless flights commence;
Slow-toned the cow-bell, and sad whippoorwill
Mourned in her darkling copse behind the hill.
Then when the tasks of ev'ning all were done,
Around the blazing hearth new sports begun;
When corn was pestled for the next day's meals,
The bands were slackened on their cumb'rous wheels,
The woodsman from his labor had come home
And plowmen from their furrows wearysome;
Loud glee pursued the "blind man" round and round,
Till roaring laughter tripped him to the ground.
The "old gray witch," slow-motioned, then would stare,
While the gay rompers felt a secret scare,—
Went crouching from her, dodged from wall to wall,
Or in the corners scrambling, tumbled all.
Thus poured the murmuring tide of childish mirth,
While sober converse leaned around the hearth,
And weighty matters in each earnest breast,

Beguiling time, prolonged the way to rest.
Oh happy times of man's innocency!
When earth was as like Heaven as could be,
When simple relish made each sport more dear,
Delayed the seasons and prolonged the year.

Within yon rude-built pile with gables gray,
With which the wanton blasts of Winter play,
When all disconsolate they moan and fret,
The simple council of the village met.
Where mutual interests called them to consult
Life's surest course, and probable result.
Hark! yon small rusty bell shakes from its throat
A few slow sounds, the assembling hour to note.
No *paid* men patriotic speeches make,
No brazen instruments their music wake,
Nor pages pass their sparkling draughts around,
And yet the weight of policies profound,
Burdens each breast, and doctrines pure and sound,
Consult a future *people's* liberties,
Without the pomp of courtly vanities.
Their theme the building of a colony,
Their views as various as their interests be,
The past is traversed with a sober gaze,
Truths gathered from experience's ways,
And probabilities dexterously thrown
In Reason's scales, to balance up or down.
Suggestions follow; till each one in turn,
His neighbor's leading views succeeds to learn.
Discussion then proceeds, orderly, clear,
Each member striving simplest to appear,
And each assuming rather to be taught,
Than teach the other, e'en if teach he ought.
If different grounds their judgments mild divide,
Each yields his own to take the other's side;
Or, if one holds a point at one's expense,
He argues only in his point's defense,
And not *against* the others, shows how plain
His views are to discover his friend's gain.

Thus order o'er the council all prevails,
And harshness ne'er reflection's ear assails.
So when some peaceful stream pursues its course
Down moaning falls and rapids gurgling hoarse,
Each separate object finds a tongue distinct,
But all together blend, and each in one's extinct.

These names were chief in council: 'Squire Grimes,
A stern Lycurgus of the backwoods times,
And pious parson Deems, of honored name,
And mild Sir Maxey of lineal fame.
A man of little more than medium size
Was he, with soft brown hair and hazel eyes,
A light gray even beard, an open face,
An easy carriage, and a happy trace
Of deep reflection in his general mien,
That e'en by dull observers might be seen.
Unlike the Cæsar of a forest shed,
To daring deeds, and frontier perils bred,
So sensitive his elevated mind,
For combat and disaster too refined,
At bloody sights a horror seized his breath,
And fears swum thro' his veins at thought of death.
And such is man, to different fortunes born;
When different schools his early life adorn,
A hero dwindles to a merest lout
When nothing calls the latent hero out.

The name of Gabriel Grimes, whene'er one spoke,
The thought of law immediately awoke.
His *mien meant* law, his voice and his attire,—
In truth the very man seemed born a 'Squire.
Not tall was he but round, and fat and tan,
And twice as thick as any other man.
Reserved, yet free, incautious, yet alert,
He suffered ne'er his character a hurt
By weightless talk. When others laughed he'd frown,
When others frowned he'd laugh, and so renown,
E'en as the jackal hunts the lion down,

Ran after him all frothy mouthed; and praise
Sounded her horn at his peculiar ways.
'Twas granted all the depths of law he knew,
For what he *did* know, others ne'er saw thro'.
His strength lay not in doing mighty things,
But giving mighty inferences wings,
And thus it is with many great of earth,
Not what they are, but what we think them worth.

But David Deems, his opposite in all,
Was pleasant, candid, unassuming, tall.
A cloud of fleecy locks hung peacefully
About his neck, according happily
With his broad look of open charity,
And ever in his careful placid face
The sweet light shone of vital inward grace,
Like dawnings of a better world—no glare
Of hot ambitions e'er ascending there,
Nor earth's polluting fires. His was no mien
Of sanctity affected, while between
His precepts and his practice, regions lay
Untraversed in his life; but as the day,
The cloudless lustre of his zealous soul
Beamed solid forth, and held in mute control,
Or stirred with song-cheer all within his reach.
He practiced how to live as well as preach,
And when he prayed, "Our debtors be forgiven,"
His soul and mind and strength conversed with Heaven,
Denouncing sin, the rebel, trembling heard,
And breathless hung upon his lightest word;
Describing bliss, wretchedness raised her eyes,
And with his lifted hand assayed to rise,
To spurn cold earth and dwell beyond the skies.
But when with pity streaming down his cheek,
The pierced bleeding Lamb of God, so meek
He pointed to, loud sobs responsive told
What sway o'er hearts a godly man may hold.
Ah, God! for more such in these turbid days,
Who preach to save souls, not to win mere praise,

Who walk *with* men to lead them out of vice,
And cause them to secure the "pearl of price."

'Twas then fair Saville that thy just renown
Was trumpeted in all the pride of town.
For all the hunting stations far and near,
Thou wast a depot to all hunters dear.
The tide of immigration drifting e'er,
Far on thy desert shores, some pioneer;
Soon far around, in distant wilds unknown,
Rude lodges from adventurer's hands were strewn,
And Husbandry went forth with sturdy hand,
To clear the waste and dress a prosperous land.
The voice of cleavers in yon valleys wide,
Were heard from breaking morn till eventide;
Loud rang their sudden axes blow on blow,
Deep thro' the waste re-echoed from below,
Great trees came crashing with a thundering sound,
Heaved from their stumps, and groaned along the ground.

Lo! in the mountains where yon wild cascade
Leaps thro' the sun and trembles in the shade,
Or sings in the sad ear of loneliness;
Where noteless birds come in the drowsiness
Of pulseless Summer's unremitting heat,
Where o'er the stream the forest branches meet,
Where rocks oppose the climber's sterile way—
And gorges yawn beneath in rugged gray,
High in the seat of Ancient Solitude,
The border woodsman rears his cabin rude.
Equipped with rifle, axe, and faithful dogs,
Here dwells the sovereign of a hut of logs;
By one attended of the fearless fair,
A consort in the wilds well worth his care.

By day the husband ventures forth for food,
Far from his lodge, within some friendly wood;
At eve returning to that constant one,
Who dared to bide his coming all alone.

Then when the twilight spreads her mantle pale
O'er wood and hill, and darkens in the vale,
His axe, and ready loaded gun near by,
His watchful mastiffs snugly napping nigh,
The window latched, and stoutly barred the door,
The day's adventures are recounted o'er.
The bear is now pursued over fallen logs,
Opposed by these, and pressed by eager dogs,
The herd's seen pouring thro' the startled dell,
The fleet stag's shot and hung up where he fell.
Thus on, the current of narration flows,
Deeper and deeper wearing as it goes,
Till heavy slumber settles on their eyes;
Converse moves sluggish, thoughts slower arise,
And faint and fainter flick'ring, sink the rays,
That wander from the fagot's dying blaze,
Till embers pale surviving—nothing more,
Light them to rest to dream their chattings o'er.

Look where yon hunters two or three or more,
The solitary wilds to westward now explore.
Thro' mountain paths, by lakes and streams they roam,
The woods their dwelling-place, the world their home!
In beast skins clad, dark jungles wind they thro',
With eager strides their desert way pursue,
And with wild pleasure gaze on every prospect new.
At times hopelessly lost these wandered long,
The hostile tribes of savages among.
By day their only show of safety
Their excellence in sylvan strategy.
The wild bird's song seemed as a mournful tale,
And e'en a twig's fall turned their faces pale;
And every little throat did omens bear,
That shocked their senses with a seige of fear,
Till restless hunger whetted valor keen,
And dared the perils of the dismal scene.
When thro' the darkling bosom of the dell
The footsteps of the cautious ranger fell
In measured silence on the Indian trail,

And fierce alarm was tongued by every gale;
When streamed the burning wigwam's lurid light
Against the forest walls of troubled night,
And quick-eyed dragoons threaded every pass,
O'er mountain rocks, and in the deep morass,
Then cougar-footed strategy slunk in
Before the lion tread of Discipline.

For these, fair Saville, these frontiersmen bold,
Whose praise in song or story ne'er was told,
For these, thou wast a haven where all turned,
And where for all a genial hearth e'er burned.
When fugitives to this free home of ours,
Sought liberty beneath thy Western bowers;
From shores whence bigotry, with flaming hand,
Expelled poor conscience naked from the land,
Pale wanderers flocked to thee in many a trembling band.

From torpid Norway's habitations drear,
Where Summer smiles to soothe the frigid year
In vain, and boisterous, railing torrents moan
The bitter discord of their cheerless zone,
And wintry blasts o'er naked landscapes shriek,
While sparse fed herds migrate from peak to peak
In dismal groups, to browse the thawing slope,
Or huddle in the drowsy mountain cope;
From fair Italia's hills of evergreen,
O'er-canopied in stillest blue serene,
From fields where Summer plants her fragrant train
Beside the lucent streamlets of the plain;
From old determined Britain (Britian); morose Wales—
Where life's as stately as a ship with sails—
From Scotia's genial bourne of soul and song,
Where poverty, though simple, spurns the wrong,
Where love and labor meet fraternally;
Fair land of Burns and wand'ring minstrelsy;
From Germany's wide realms of smoke and beer,
Where dreamy metaphysics sits austere;
From over-flowing, ever-bowing France,

The home of fashions, fopperies and dance;
From sacred Judah, and beyond the Nile,
And from priest-ridden Erin's suppliant isle,
Escaping bands from Famine, Tyranny
And Ignorance, fled here for liberty.
A home for empty indigence was here;
The broken spendthrift found a friendly sphere,
The hopeless suiter came in all his throes,
To sport away the burdens of his woes;
Here wealth and romance found a fit abode,
And hand-in-hand with fame and fancy strode;
Ambition, in his sanguinest career,
Found a theatre for his conquests here;
And grave philanthropy, advising stood,
Disposed to do the unborn future good;
And here apostles of the hidden life
Implored kind Heaven to hold the winds of strife,
Pronounced swift judgment on transgression's ways,
Encouraged virtue, recommended praise,
Enlivened hope, taught faith to patient be,
Cheered manly toil and lauded charity.

With strongest cords of mutual interest bound,
All hands together were employed found.
Engaged to arm against a common foe,
The strength of unity they learned to know;
And what convenience Art had them denied,
United, willing hands full well supplied.
They reared their cabins, built their forest forts
Together, hunted, fished and held their sports.
The sick they joined to nurse with sleepless care,
To soothe the suffering, knew no pains to spare,
And when from earth the patient spirit fled,
They joined their mournful tributes to the dead.
Thus plenty flourished on the lap of ease,
And even danger's self was made to please.
Bold industry at hardships learned to smile,
Uproot vast wants and hew down woods of toil.
So when the forest matron crowned her board

With health and sustenance from her good hoard,
The unknown wanderer had a welcome there,
And indolence was e'en allowed a chair.
Lo! where yon woodsman skirts the neighboring weald,
And nears his smoking cot behind the field.
His step aweary quickens at each pace,
And satisfaction lightens his tired face
As home he views; Home! isle in time's rough sea,
Where rests the voyager serene and free
From hollow, howling sorrows, that surround
His rock, and shake life's groaning depths profound—
Where winds repose, in long unruffled peace,—
Dear isle! where love's bright shine doth never cease—
And where no sooner doth the bloomy train,
Their sweetness drop, than blooms revive again.
Lo, now the evening star in grandeur still
Ascends yon upland wood and sheep cote hill,
Like some pale maiden at the trysting late,
Hard thro' the twilight peering o'er the gate;
The loud cur at the hollow nightfall bays,
And whispers flutter round the bright hearth's blaze,
Then nearer draws the rustic to his seat,
His warming heart outstrips his hasting feet;
All day his manly arms to labor bared,
Have wrought the task, returning want prepared.
Blest be the man, who void of all pretense,
Repays in ample sweat kind Providence,
For all His goods, and great beneficence!
And blest the consort of his lusty cares,
Who seeks his pleasures and his labor shares.
Behold the pilgrim leaning at their door,
Water he begs and shelter—nothing more;
The frowning wealth of some far distant land,
Has driven him to leave with empty hand.
See how the wond'ring little ones apprise
Their busy mother with their sparkling eyes.
She to the stranger bows, extends a chair,
And chides her bright-eyed cherubs if they stare.
Hark! now the cotter's well-known steps draw near,

And patter faster as the stile they clear.
Soon in the door appears his open face,
A flock of kisses fly to his embrace;
The smaller, raised upon his manly breast,
Chirp out, and crow, and carrol at the rest.
And the kind housewife, hasty to obey
A tender conscience, happy seems as they.
Her eyes upon the hoary stranger bent,
Speak her desire, and ask her lord's consent.
All signs and looks unpleasant are repressed,
And ample supper set before their guest;
Who, having vanquished potent hunger quite,
Is kindly *pressed* upon to stay all night!
Blest be the man! his hands arrest his wants,
His charity is great, but never vaunts.
He now to quiet night's embrace repairs,
And sleeps away his weariness and cares.
Sweet be the visions of his manly breast,
Nor by remorseful dreams of wealth, nor banished joys opprest.

These were the mighty days of little things,
Ere soaring vanity had yet her wings.
For gain was satisfied with but his own.
Then aspirations of the noblest kind,
Dear humble comfort to her hights confined.
These were the good old times of simple worth,
When love and reverence met at every hearth;
When strong toil stretched beneath green plenty's tree,
And worshipped home's best god dear Industry.
Then gaunt-armed indiscretion, pale and sore,
Groaning beneath disease's dreaded sting
Through sleepless hours, was never known. The king
Most terrible of all the hordes of bale,
Intemp'rance, did not then the peace assail
Of hopeful hearts, breathing out crime and hate,
And houseless want and hearths all desolate.
Then blushing beauty's cheek of tender hues,
Showed not excessive drink and what ensues.
Ah! fatal days of wantonness and wine,

In which *now* youthful wealth assays to shine,
Deriding with the jeers of native glee,
The homespun customs of their ancestry!
Regarding lights which made our land sublime,
As smouldering embers on the hearth of time.
In wilds remote from fame's resounding horn,
Where courts were never dreamed of, kings were born,
Or minds that might have worn star-gemmed renown,
And added lustre to a James' crown
With all the sovereign claims of Royalty,
Wisdom, valor, and sterling honesty.
The way from office then was hedged by fines,
The way to office *now* by party lines.
Oh, God! for a return to simple ways,
Such as crowned Saville in her valiant days,
Ere yet the pluming warrior's barb'rous knife
Cut down the flower on the lap of life!

But, Saville, pause! for God's sake pause! I beg!
For thy fair bosom warms a viper's egg.
The hatching ruin will thy young life sting,
And pour a deadly poison thro' thy nature's spring.
Thou hold'st one slave! Of barbarisms old
An evil seed now in thy life takes hold.

Prosperity's big rain to cheer thee falls,
And plenty overhangs thy garden walls;
Soft blooming gladness in thy hedges peep,
And green delight doth at thy waysides creep,
Contentment murmurs in thy valleys low,
And health's rejoicing streams from fruitful hillsides flow;
But Justice n'er can say, "peace be in thee,"
While one beneath thy grinding heel pants to be free.
Ah! can'st thou hold the life of one in chains,
With eighty-five per cent. of Saxon in his veins?
Oh, Saville, look at what a crime thy nature stains!

Thy Rodney, see, how noble he appears,
Just on the summit of his tender years!

His Summers number scarce a single score,
And yet his manly face seems marked by more.
When pity calls, his brawny arm assumes
A woman's softness, and as light becomes.
But when the right enlists him to oppose,
On whate'er grounds, whatever of her foes,
His face as gentle as a sleeping child's,
Would dare the fury of the roaring wilds;
His nerves put on their fearless strength, and steeled
By valor stern, the knife or rifle wield.
Erect in air he stands full six-feet, three,
Broad shouldered, strong, a goodly man is he.
A lover of fair women, and as blind
To her weaknesses as Egyptian night,
A fondler with soft childhood, and as kind
To its mistakes, as if mistakes were right;
Skilled in the feats that backwoods life adorn,
Although a stranger to the backwoods born,
The shelly clamor of the Autumn trees,
Or howl of beasts, or savages alike can please.
And he a slave? Ah, Saville, can it be

The Old Sac Village

Ye who read in musty volumes
Pages worn of Backwoods Times,
Of the red man and the white man,
In the thrilling days of danger,
In the gall of border troubles,
In the wastes of deadly revenge,
And the ruffian hands of torture;
And of long and fierce death grapples,
With the bloody hands of combat,
On the yawning edge of famine;
Of adventure's rustling footsteps,
When the knees of stoutest valor
Smote together as they paused, where
Lynx-eyed strategy lay crouching,
On the bosom of still ambush,
Ready from his hands to let loose
A loud leash of swift cruelties;
Ye who read these musty volumes,
Till a strange sensation thrills you,
As of Indians skulking near you,
Lay aside your volume lightly,
Hear me sing of Nanawawa.

Ye who pore for weary hours,
In the deep wild nooks of legend,

In the forest-nooks of legend,
Gath'ring up these strange old relics,
For your idle thoughts to play with;
Such as wigwams rude, and war posts,
Belts of wampum, bows and arrows,
Scalping-knives, and rough stone hatchets,
Peace pipes and great council fires,
Forest senates, and wise treaties,
Forest seers and superstitions,
And inconstancy and cunning,

In the savage world of promise;
Ye who pore for weary hours
In these pathless nooks of legend,
Wake, and hear of Nanawawa.

Ye who wander long delighted,
In the distant realms of romance,
On the mountain hights of romance,
And in woody depths of romance,
Getting lost in shady windings,
Looking not to find your way out,
But a wood to wander off in,
And a nook to lose yourselves in;
With majestic trees around you,
Clasping in their arms of grandeur,
Densest depths of sleeping silence,
Clear, deep, still lakes, on whose margins
Peaceful herds feed, dreams the heron,
On whose bosoms swift and light glide
Birch canoes, arrowy darting,
Like soft shadows, smooth and soundless;
Floating thro' unbroken stillness,
Save the distant fret of oar-locks,
And the pebbly speech of bright waves;
Ye who seek these depths of romance,
Where the noon-beam parts the fore locks
Of the forest looking shyly,
Where a thousand wind-swung branches,
Wild songs pour in Solitude's ear,
And the heart of meditation
Slowly beats and warms in beating;
Pause, and hear of Nanawawa.

Ye who shut up in warm houses,
Late on sombre Winter evenings,
Lulled by pleasant roaring grate fires,
And the cozy flap of curtains,
And the chirp of vacant childhood,
And the cheery streams of gaslight

Meekly stealing, that pause, bashful,
On the plushy lap of softness;
Ye who thus shut up in houses,
Dream of early life and hardships,
Shut in humble frontier cabins,
Far out on the unknown borders;
Dream of weariness o'ercoming

The lost traveler on his journey
Overtaken by the snow-storm;
Lone at night and his path dimming,
Sinking down to sleep his death sleep;
Chilly leagues from any dwelling,
And while loneliness bewails him,
Through the drear woods shrieks the gray blast,
Shrieks the eager flying North blast,
As a hungry eagle shrieketh;
Ye who shut up thus in houses,
Dream of these fell border hardships;
Hear me sing of Nanawawa.
Ah! ye shall behold a beauty!
On the lap of an old forest,
In the wigwam of her fathers,
By the cascades of her childhood
Ye shall see a sylvan maiden,
Meek as April's first fresh rose is,
Sweet as blushing light e'er looked on,
Brilliant as a melting dewdrop,
But in love pensively youthful.

In the days that long ere these times,
Went their way with loud importance,
On the thrilling lips of warfare,
And the tongue of backwoods valor,
Told to many generations;
There was a rude Indian village,

Far within a glen sequestered,
In the basin of a clear brook,

Near the waters of the Wabash,
In the Mississippi valley.
In this ancient birch bark village,
With his daughter, Nanawawa,
Dwelt the chief of all the Sac tribes,
Old and austere Pashepaho,
Powerful and warlike Stabber.
On a hill, the Stabber's tent stood
High above the other lodges,
And the goodliest among them.
Once upon the moon of bright nights,
On a day in budding April,
At his tent door sat the Stabber,
With his chin leaned on his hands, sat
Knitting thoughts above his sage brow,
And pursuing speculations,
Through the sober depths of study.
"What a brilliant sun-set," said he,
As the world of quiet West woods
Slowly reddened into amber,
And the sunset-spangled clouds threw
Up their long arms tipped with fire,
And sank down in sleepy glory,
In a deep still sea of glory.
"Sing a camp song, Nanawawa,"

"I will help you sing it over."
Said he, turning to his daughter.
"On the morrow is the full moon,
And the great feast of the Sac tribes,
When the Chiefs of all the nations
Will come in to see the Stabber
And report upon the country.
They will tell me of their huntings,
And of fishings in their clear streams,
Of their pleasant sugar makings,
And of fields of green maize growing;
They will tell of wild adventures
With the bear and with the bison,

And will tell the great traditions
Of their tribes and of their totems.
Goodly presents they will bring me,
Venison to make the feast with,
Bear skins to adorn my tent with,
Paints to make my old age youthful,
Beads to brighten favor's dull eyes,
Wampum to revive old friendships,
And great words to move the heart with.

"Sing a camp song, Nanawawa,
Sing until the time of sleep comes,
I will join and help you sing it."
Nanawawa sang a camp song,
And the Stabber joined the singing,

Till asleep they sat and sang yet,
Till they went to sleep a singing.
Morning came, and as the hours
Went their way, they brought crowds with them,
Of the distant tribes and totems.
Noon approached, and saw the great feast,
In its highest wild demeanor,
In the savage hights of ardor.
Eating, drinking, gaming, dancing,
Mingled in a ceaseless whirling
To the sound of forest music.
Evening came, and as the feast sank
To repose, as sinks the warrior
On his shield, of fields aweary
And the long parade of armies,
To the tent door of the Stabber,
Chieftains came and stood in silence.
Pashepaho in his tent floor,
On his bear skins sat a smoking.
Not a word said he to any,
But a seat he motioned them to,
And went dryly on a smoking
As they settled close around him.

Young men, chiefs of the Ojibways,
The Miamis, and Dacotahs,
And the mighty Sacs and Foxes,
Laid their presents rare and costly,

At the Stabber's feet; and seated
On their armor, in great phrases
Of their forest tongues, made speeches.
On her tent floor, Nanawawa
Looking not upon the young men,
Heard their sounding words of valor.
Tho' the eyes of great chiefs sought her,
She would starve their eager glances,
Turning from them on the tent floor.

Pashepaho's Speech to the Young Men

Pashepaho heard the young men
Till their lofty words had ended,
And in accents stern, thus answered:
"For your presents, I am thankful.
By your speeches I'm encouraged.
Peace now lighteth all the Nations
As a noon sun lights the prairies.
Time once was when peace was broken
Up in all our Western borders.
Horsed on fire, bloody battle
Rode throughout our ancient forests.
From his home within the sunrise,
From his land of bells and steeples,
From the regions of the East wind,
The hoar dwelling place of Wabun,
Then Spake the Great Father to us,
To his red tribes spake in loud tones
As of thunder in the forests.
"Now be peaceable, my children,
Dwell in friendship's tents together,
You, my red sons and my white sons."
Then he took his great war hatchet,
That could strike with blows of thunder,

And into the mountains wandered,
Went forth in the deepest valleys,
And at one blow hewed a pine down,
Fell a great pine of the valleys,
That looked upward into Heaven,
With the East winds in his left hand,
And the West winds in his right hand,
And the noon-beams in his forelocks;
Took this old pine of the valleys,
And to make a war-post, reared it.
Then he spake again, in this wise:
"Lo! the war-post now ascendeth!

See the war-post of the nations,
Now the Great Spirit beholds it;
See it pointing into Heaven
Like the finger of a giant!
Bury now your hatchets neath it,
And be peaceable my children,
Dwell in friendship's tents together."
Then the sky above the war-post,
Grew as clear as any crystal,
And the dreamy air was softened,
And the dazing blue seemed higher,
And the far off hills seemed farther,
And all sounds were low and solemn.
Then the red sons and the white sons,
Neath the war-post sat together.

When the red sons spake in this wise:
"Raise your eyes and look now, brothers,
See it now is Indian Summer.
Lo! the sky is all serene now,
And the hills are all a sleeping,
How the brown woods now are yawning?
Now the slow streams sing in whispers.
And the South wind passeth softly
In her moccasins of damp moss.
Lo! this now is Indian Summer,
And the time to go a hunting.
We will leave you now, and hasten
To the mountains for a bear hunt.
Our light canoes are waiting
By the waters. Brothers, farewell.
Then spake the Great Father to us,
As we stood beside the waters,
By the moorings of our canoes,
And shook-hands with all our brothers.

"Thus your hunting grounds, my red sons,
Shall extend; my white sons know them.
From Kaskaskia to Cahokia,

From St. Vincennes to St. Louis,
Up the Wabash, Illinois,
The Wisconsin, and Great Water,
To the regions of the North wind,
Where the bold St. Lawrence spreadeth

Out the fingers of his right hand;
Where the dun moose snuffs the lake fog,
Snuffs the cold breath of the North Lakes,
And the slow bear baffles Winter,
In his sullen reign of deep snows;
Where the son of Giant waters
Rocks the earth as in a cradle,
And sings lullabys of thunder
In the ear of old Forever,
Till the darkness sighs and shudders,
And the white hills quake and whisper,
"Lo, Niagara is waking!"
From this birth-place of the hoar blasts,
To the wigwam of the South wind,
In the myriad-voiced prairies,
Where the wild goose sounds her pibroch,
And the wild duck talks her nonsense,
And the heron shoots her slant flights,
From her dreamings in the long grass;
These shall be—then loud he uttered—
Hunting grounds for you forever."
Then said Pashepaho, turning
From his audience, and smoking,
"Peace now lighteth up our forests,
And our wigwams all are cheerful."

Nanawawa's Suitors

When the Stabber's speech had ended,
And his presents all were gathered,
And his pipe the chiefs had all smoked,
Four young chiefs of goodly mein, came
Round the princess of the forest,
And upon the tent floor kneeling,
Made obesience to her lowly.
Then they rose and gave *her* presents,
Costly beads and many colored
One presented, one a necklace
Of rare stones, one silver brooches
For her hair, and one gold wristlets.
All then went and sat in silence,
Waiting for the maiden's answer.
Pausing, seemed the maid more pretty.
Youthful seemed in indecision.
At the presents looked and suitors,
Looked at one and then the others.
Ah! how lovely now her soft eyes
Shone as her young hands grew doubtful.
Fairest daughter of the wigwams,
Blithest warbler of the deep shades,
Sweetest flower that e'er shined there,
Having o'er her native sweetness
Rarest hues of loneliness shed.

Ah! she was a lovely doubter!
Beads about her perfect neck hung,
Like the clusters of a ripe vine.
Wristlets clasped her naked round arms,
With reluctance seemed to clasp them,
As a lover clasps a lover.
Undecided, ah, how youthful,
Ah, how rare was Nanawawa!
Pashepaho silent sitting,
With a true parental pride, watched

His fair daughter thro' the pipe smoke
That in clouds his head environed.
At the door-way of the wigwam,
Then a chief stood, a Dacotah,
Leading a young captive with him,
A fair child of some white settler.
In the captive's face, the light shone
Of intelligence and training.
He the hopes showed of proud parents.
Long his locks, and golden, floated
To his shoulders, blue his eyes were,
And as sunbeams penetrating.
But captivity's cold buffets
Pensive made him seem and forlorn.
Then the presents of the young chiefs,
Nanawawa threw back to them,
Rose and met the young Dacotah,

Took the captive by the right hand,
And the young chief by the left hand,
And into the wigwam led them.
"Here," said she, "This is my present,
As the captive's hand she held to,
Give me this lad for a present."
"I have brought him for your present,"
Sighed the hopeful young Dacotah.
Thus it was that Nanawawa
Found a lover in her wigwam,
Found a husband at her door-way.
For within her heart she whispered,
In her heart the thought she uttered,
"I have found a husband surely."
But a secret hid she kept it,
Though she to her own heart told it,
Pashepaho never knew it.
Many days in happiness dwelt
Nanawawa and the captive;
For the Stabber took the captive,
Smeared his face with many colors,

Hung his golden locks with brooches,
Armed him with a bow and arrows,
And his son, the White Loon, named him;
Nanawawa's brother called him.
Meanwhile all the village loved him,
Loved young Nanawawa's brother.

In their huntings and their fishings,
All the young men of the village
Sought companionship in White Loon.
For the deer hunt he was ready,
For the bison chase and bear hunt;
And when Spring had warmed the rivers,
And their flow from mountains quickened,
On the bosom of the full tide,
His canoe was seen with others.
He was called the lucky fisher.
Thus it was that in the Sac town,
White Loon grew to be admired.
And at every tent door pausing,
In the morning or the evening,
Groups of cheerful faces met him,
With their dusky smiles of welcome.
Old men talked of him with wise looks,
And the young with brightened faces.
Children spoke of him in whispers,
And with little looks of wonder,
Grouped behind him in the tent doors;
For to them he was a prophet.
He could tell of ghosts and genii,
In the woods and in the waters;
In the rolling Susquehanah,
And the broad and rapid Hudson,
And the blue and peaceful Huron,

He could tell of evil genii,
Clasping hands upon the waters,
And to elfin music dancing
On the clear and moonlit waters.

Thus it was he told the children
Of a proud and faithless lover,
And the genii of the waters,
On the dark shores of Lake Huron.
"In a land of lakes and great woods,
In a green and distant country,
On the high cliffs of Lake Huron,
High as two pine trees together,
In a wigwam of great oak trees,
Lived a mighty chief of white men.
Old the man, and long his beard was
As the bow string of a warrior.
Long his hair, and thick and white was,
Like the pine's locks in a snow storm.
This chief had a lovely daughter.
Light was she, and full of sunshine,
And her words were all as cheerful
As a stream that glideth onward.
And her songs were all as buoyant
As the loud songs of a cascade.
In her speech music of groves was,
In her hair the gold of sunset,
In her cheek the blush of sunrise,

On her brow the shade of twilight,
In her eyes the blue of soft skies;
And her teeth were rows of pearl beads.
This fair squaw a young chief once loved,
And her hand in marriage promised.
But her heart was light and wayward,
And smiled on him, but went from him,
Till his eyes were mooned in frenzy,
And he fell into Lake Huron.
From the high cliffs that looked downward
From behind the great oak wigwam,
Genii, dancing on the lake's breast,
Saw him fall, and seized him sinking,
And with shouts of music, bore him
To a land beneath the waters.

Night by night then came his lover
To the bluffs behind her wigwam,
And long hours in the moonlight
Gazed down on the sleepy waters.
Thus she thought once when she went there:
"Oh! I'm sorry! I am sorry!
Since he's gone; Oh, now I'm sorry!
Could he hear me in his dark grave
Of the frightful rocking billows,
I would say to him, forgive me!
Speak, O waves, for now your hoarse words
Breaking on the rocks may tell me!

Can he hear my heart lamenting?"
Now the genii heard her sorrows,
Formed a circle of enchantment,
And upon the billows seated,
Filled the ravished air with sweet sounds;
Till the fair squaw, like her lover,
Fell among them, and they seized her,
And away with laughter bore her,
In the blue and silent Huron.
Now within the land of shadows,
Far beneath the sad still Huron,
In the deep home of the genii,
These two lovers are seen riding
E'er behind two harnessed moonbeams."
And of giants in the mountains,
White Loon also told the children.
Thus he told them of the giants:
"In a land of pines and great rocks,
In a far off land of mountains,
In the gateway of the sunrise,
Where the East wind shakes the door latch
On the wigwam of the sunrise.
There were giants in the old days;
Giants tall as mountain pine trees.
When it stormed upon the mountains,
And the woods were black with terror

And their speech was low and dismal,
Then, when thunders rolled and rumbled
On the stony streets of Heaven;
In the wigwams of the valleys.
Sat the stoutest warriors trembling,
And in whispers low and fearful
Muttered, 'Listen at the giants!
Ugh, the giants now are angery,
And will tear the very hills down!'"
Thus it was that White Loon's wisdom
Made him to his friends a prophet.

Nanawawa's Lakelet

Where the dark ash upward towereth,
And the maple drops her brown shade,
And the rough oak spreads his broad arms,
And the wild vine weaves her festoons;
Where the noon breeze pants for sunlight,
And the sunbeams wandereth shyly,
And the night-winds wrestleth lightly,
With the lone leaf of the forest;
Where the moon-beams creepeth softly,
In a dim veil looking faintly;
In this ancient grand high forest,
In the right hand of Kaskaskia,
And the left hand of Cahokia,
And the regions of the Wabash;
Was the little rush bound lakelet,
Of the forest—Nanawawa's.
Tall trees in the solemn old woods,
On the western slopes and hilltops,
Threw their shadows in the bottoms.
Parting ferns and water-lilies,
And the rushes, that with wet lips
Sipped the lakelet's clear, cool waters;
Nanawawa's birch canoe flashed
Light and noiseless as the shadow
Of a cloud upon a meadow.
In this fleet canoe sat White Loon,

But the oars held Nanawawa,
And the boat plied with her bare arms,
And to White Loon talked in whispers.

Now a moon rose o'er the forest
Of the great Northwestern Country,
And looked down into the lakelet
As a maid looks in her mirror.
All the air was in a slumber,

And the forests, in a deep nap,
Breathed not as soft light stole o'er them,
Wrapt in fleecy garb of thin mists,
Night had gently closed her eyelids,
Clasping all the world in silence;
Save the creek that in the lake leapt,
Coming from the wooded hillside,
Saying strange things to the clear moon.
As the boat flashed thro' the moonlight,
White Loon near to Nanawawa
Drew his face, and spoke in this wise:
"White Loon loves you, Nanawawa!"
When these words fell, both her oars fell,
And she upward at the moon gazed,
With both hands dropped in the water.
As the forest maiden's soul swam
In her eyes, White Loon leaned o'er her,
Drew her naked bosom to him,
Drew her to him close and listened;

With his breathings half suspended,
Listened to her words of music
Dropping like a wasted shower
Thro' the leafy depths of Autumn;
"Nanawawa loves you, White Loon,
"White Loon you must build a wigwam."
White Loon raised his eyes and answered:
"By yon cascade in the mountains,
High above the village looking,
I will build my great birch wigwam,
Ere the wintry hours approacheth."
And his heart with aspen lightness
Turned toward a happy future.
Forest-love brings forethought with it.
Nuptial care dwells in the wildwood;
In the Indian's poor wigwam
Love's bright sunshine casteth shadows.
Thus it was that White Loon, wooing
On the lakelet of the forests,

In the clear and placid moonlight,
Saw a happy future rising
And its pleasant tasks revealing.
Thus it was he built a wigwam,
Dressed it carefully with bear skins,
And the door adorned with stag's horns,
To abide the bridal entrance.
Then it was he went a hunting,
Went far off into the mountains,
Seeking food to meet the winter.
Saying, as he clambered onward,
With the eager warrior's hunted;
"I will soon return, I'm hoping,
Let our hunting time be short now."

DEATH OF PASHEPAHO

Lo! the old Sac village slumbered
In the basin of the Wabash,
And the doorway of the vallies,
Like some brown old matron napping
On the threshold of her cottage,
When her distaff lieth idle.
All the plaintive vale was cooing,
And the hazy hills were piping,
And the mournful gales were flapping
Thro' their somber realms of sere woods.
Sang the crane migrating southward,
Answered the itin'rant heron
In her dank and grassy rev'rie,
By the blue and pensive waters.
Then it was that sate the Stabber;

In the middle of his tent floor;
Sate with sober words and features,
Talking of the times he once knew,
Now with the departed past blent,
Now deep in the grave of years laid.
At his side sat Nanawawa,
And her voice like running waters
O'er a pebbly bed descanting,
Sank upon his ears with rapture;
With a wild and lonely rapture,
As she asked him of the old times.
"Nanawawa," said he, trembling,
"You had better take a husband.
From the great tribes of the west plains,
Take a strong and valiant young chief,
For I soon must go and leave you.
From the wigwam of your mother,
Sixteen years ago you followed;
From the lone spot where we left her,
Where the mournful vine entwines her,

Where the wild briar blooms above her,
Where the wild birds sing unto her;
From that spot I love to think of,
Sixteen years ago you followed
To this wide and unknown country.
Since that time you've e'er been with me,
E'er been sunlight in my tent door,

Ever been the joy of old age;
But my daughter, Oh! my daughter,
Oh! my hind, my Nanawawa!
I am now upon a journey,
And you *now* cannot go with me!"
Nanawawa could not answer,
And for tears saw not the Stabber,
As he leaned upon the tent floor,
And went on to utter faintly:
"What is that I hear a coming?
Don't I hear the sound of footmen
Coming from a distant country?
Ah! I hear the tread of warriors,
They are coming in a hurry!
I behold great lands before me,
Now I see green mountains rising,
And I see the peaceful wigwams,
Just across the river yonder!
Nanawawa, I must leave you!
Come and see me in the morning.
Oh! my daughter, come and see me!"
Nanawawa caught her father,
Stooping o'er him, called and called him,
Pressed his face against her pale cheek,
Held his hands and watched his still lips.
Then a wail burst from the wigwam;
Pashepaho had ceased breathing!

SAVILLE IN TROUBLE

Sing muse! of Saville and the direful day
When beauty fell, to ruthless hands a prey;
And life a sacrifice to savage hate,
Smoked on the alter of a peaceful State.
The pensive forest in his saddest wear,
Leaned on the threshold of the Autumn sere,
And mourned his ills in parting Summer's ear.
And waters leaving for the distant main
Sang their departure in a muffled strain.
The dove complaining at the barn was heard,
In wanton gales the naked orchards stirred.
And scarce within the dreamy vision's reach
The sheep cote elms flapped their rocky speech.
In Saville, then, the border village rude,
Full plenty's songs the ear of labor wooed,
And lulled him on the lap of solitude.
The sun had swum high on his blazoned way,
Exulting in the power of his sway.
And rural comfort's well-contented hum,
Rejoiced in each household cherrysome.
The milkmaid gossipped at her busy churn,
The groaning windlass coughed at each slow turn,
The distaff whirred and chattered in the door,
The swift brooch danced along the sounding floor;

The matron scolded, and her hands applied,
The loom reechoed and the wheel replied.
Sir Maxey then, with horns, and hunters proud,
For chase assembled in a roaring crowd.
The champing horses pawed the anxious ground,
And windy signals roused the kenneled hound.
And as the mingling bands their saddles strode,
The wayside trembled and deep groaned the road.
Three miles from Saville, in the branchy West,
The horsemen on their boist'rous way had pressed,
When on the wild marge of a pathless wood,

Whey reined their speed, and, list'ning, eager stood.
The hounds had touched a trail upon the brink,
Where late an antlered stag had come to drink,
And cool, within the windings of a brook,
That mused away thro' many a forest nook.
Soon lively baying o'er the distance broke,
The hills re-echoed and the forest spoke.
The flying pack their goodly prey had sprung,
St. Vincennes' pulseless woodlands deep among.
Like eagles flashing from the vaulted blue,
The firey steeds in level flight pursue.
In winding glens their hoofy thunders break,
And cliffs responsive all their voices wake.
Sir Maxey, putting spurs, directs the course,
And sweeps away upon his coal black horse.
His comrades follow close in lengthy file,

Wind their glad horns and prime their guns the while.
The woods before them part upon the eye,
And pass in dizzy currents as they fly;
And crouching thickets scamper as they near,
And flee together as they disappear.
Beyond the vision's bounds they thus have gone,
Up hill and down, o'er streams and on and on.
Meanwhile, alone on foot young Rodney hastes
Along a passage that divides the wastes.
Forbid to rank he cannot take his place
With mounted hunters in the merry chase.

The day wore on, and yet no tidings gave,
Of horse or hunter to the anxious slave,
Till he, despairing, turned to watch a trail,
That saunteringly wound along the vale.

The chase now hushed; the stag beyond his range,
Had lost his loud pursuers in a forest strange;
Till worn and hungry, these leisurely drew
To where small fenceless fields adorned their view.
Beyond, bark lodges here and there were seen,

Where lofty woods climbed o'er a long ravine.
And slowly nearing, on their wond'ring eyes,
Soft circling smoke-wreathes from a village rise,
And float in dreamy banks against the peaceful skies.
They pause, look onward, know not what to say,
When thus, Sir Maxey, spurring, leads the way:
"Come on, we'll venture down and ask for food

And friendship in this city of the wood."
The hunters follow at a timid pace,
And apprehension kindles in each face.

They reach the village, slowly thro' it ride,
And every part explore from side to side.
They find it is deserted by all save
Small groups of children and the aged brave.
These sit in converse at their wigwam doors,
While memory the valiant past explores.
They on the neighb'ring slopes in peaceful plays,
Their numbers gather and their voices raise.
The squaws are lab'ring in their scanty fields,
Content with what their wild industry yields;
To bide their warriors' much desired return
From distant hunting grounds and long sojourn.

The Autumn hills appear in brown repose,
And, clothed in lofty forests, seem to dose.
And solitude asserts her reign, remote
From civilization's rest-disturbing throat.
But, hoofy 'larm the woody silence breaks,
The lone boughs flutter and the scene awakes.
Around the hunters, childhood flocks to gaze,
And age arising, looks in mute amaze
Upon the daring strangers, who proceed
To rifle tents, and load each ready steed
With what few skins their wintry hunt can hoard,
And swallow what poor food their empty stores afford.

The helpless fathers of the forest race
Glance fearful each into the other's face,

Pursue the pillagers with heated eyes,
And empty out their souls in frequent sighs;
While in their gath'ring frowns and gestures rude,
Wild valor overleaps decrepitude,
And such a flourish of contempt displays,
As shows that stern resentment is ablaze.
Ah! could they but recall the fleeting years,
Or backwards journey to where disappears
The dim seen past, and reach that stalwart time
When nimble life exulted in its prime;
Three-fold the numbers that their tents defile,
Would meet destruction in their conduct vile.
The hunters mount menacing as they go,
And thro' the village disappearing slow,
Betake them to the woods and brisker ride
Along the neighb'ring forest's eastern side.

There where a peaceful streamlet ambles by
Thro' dabbling ferns and gossips cheerfully
With shaggy roots that reach into the flood,
They spy a maid just bord'ring womanhood.
Now ranging feathers in her head-gear fair,
And with her fingers combing out her hair,
She on the prone bank stands, where smoothly flows
The liquid mirror, and her beauty shows.
Now grand old sylvans raise their solemn heads,

And make obesience as she lightly treads
Beneath their outstretched arms, and looks around
To gather nuts upon the leaf-spread ground.
The hunters see her, wayward, wild and sweet;
She sees them not, nor hears their horses' feet.
"Hold!" cries Sir Maxey, "What a lovely maid!
Ah! what a princess of this ancient shade!
Let me behold her! Quiet! Don't move!
Did admiration e'er see such a dove?
Young love no sweeter image ever drew
Upon imagination's tender view.
Her perfect form in idle movements seems

The fleeting creature of our youthful dreams."
A rougher comrade at his elbow growls,
"A purty good 'un o' the dusky fowls,
  She's hard o' hearin', le'me try my gun;
  Give her a skere, and see the red wench run."
His deadly eye directs, his rifle speaks,
The maiden throws her arms and runs and shrieks;
Towards the hunters pitiously flies,
The mournful wastes lamenting with her cries,
Till at their feet she sinks, and all is o'er,
Poor bleeding Nanawawa is no more.

Kind Heaven reports the shameful news around,
Far as her sorrowing winds can waft the sound;
Soft echo in her grot hears with a sigh,
And saddened hills refuse to make reply.
"I struck her," grunts the ruffian, looking down,
"Let's leave," Sir Maxey mutters with a frown;
And on they ride, and covenant to keep
The crime a secret in their bosoms hidden deep.

But hark! what mean those distant shouts that rise
And seem to flap and clamor in the skies?
Flying this way, the pulseless air they wing,
And nearer, clearer, shriller, faster ring.
The forest rages, groan the loud hills sore,
The hoarse earth murmurs and the heavens roar.
Returning warriors flash the trees between;
The fatal gun has called them to the scene.
Blazing resentment fires their warlike blood,
They've passed their dwellings and enraged pursued.
And mark the hunter whom their wrath o'ertakes,
For on his head a storm of ruin breaks.
Sir Maxey's band their loud pursuers hear,
And spurring onward leave them on the rear;
For Saville wheeling quick each headlong steed,
And dash between the forests with defiant speed.
The raging warriors reach the bloody scene,
See Nanawawa lifeless on the green,

A moment pause and scan the mournful place,
Still, crafty vengeance darkening in each face,
The way the band went, narrowly then view,
And all another route at once pursue.
But one tall form his further flight restrains;

Lo! over Nanawawa's sad remains
The White Loon bends, and kisses her pale cheek,
And trembling lips that can no longer speak;
While from his eyes the streams of loud grief start,
And downwards pour the anguish of a manly heart.

As some wild wand'ring brook that surges hoarse,
And chafes and struggles in its winding course
Through tangled roots, and under mossy stones,
And over foamy cat'racts makes its moans,
Till headlong down the mountain's steepy sides,
The smoother current unobstructed glides;
Flows ev'ner as it meets the level main,
And murmurs leisurely along the plain;
So now the pluming bands their numbers drew,
In fretful streams the pathless forests thro'.
This way and that, low crouched, they galloped on,
Stood list'ning, here and there, a hight upon;
Moved down in level flight beyond the glade,
And glided into silent ambuscade;
And in the branchy covert pond'ring lay
Beside the coming hunter's thoughtless way.
As hungry cougars in the deep morass,
To seize on unsuspecting herds that pass,
Lie close and closer as their prey draws nigh,
Glance at each other with impatient eye,
And press the eager moments as they fly;
So watch these cougars of the wilderness,

And so the moment of assault they press.
With envious haste their barb'rous knives they clasp,
And poise their hatchets in a deadly grasp,
And leaning forward on their ponies wait,

Like eagles on their pinions. Coming straight
Along the gorge the hunter's chatting trot
All unsuspecting; till the fatal spot
They reach, when forth from stilly ambush nigh,
The yelling furies on their pathway fly.
Once from the tangling branches fairly freed,
Wild retribution fledges savage speed,
Straight on the hunter's right and left they wheel,
And thro' their vitals plunge the reeky steel
Swift as their iron strength the blows can deal.
All, save Sir Maxey, perish; he again
Rides through the storm like lightning to the plain,
Drives up his speed and shaves the lev'ler main.
So when fierce eagle shoots along the skies,
Breaks thro' the ambient clouds and downward flies,
Above the landscape swings his open sail,
And hangs in stately triumph o'er the vale.
Forward he leans at each successive bound,
As on and on he reaches o'er the ground.
Hard bears his courser on th' unyielding reins,
Close-scented danger swells his fiery veins,
Dilates his nostrils, to his knees inclined,
And pours their steamy volumes on the wind.

O'er log, stone, ditch, mound, shrub and brushy heaps,
Away, away he unobstructed sweeps.
In vain the heaving earth beneath him groans,
In vain the rising distance makes her moans,
In vain the wand'ring eye his flight pursues,
In vain the ear his feet receding woos;
Across their utmost limits both he shaves,
Drown'd in the roiling depths of dusty waves.
The passing gale behind him list'ning swings,
To view the rival of her speedy wings,
With breath suppressed, as when some maiden sees,
A deer go fleeting by her 'mong the trees.

Meanwhile, away behind, disheartened not,
The streaming warriors hard pursuing trot.

A.A. WHITMAN

What tho' the courser leave them like the wind?
His trail they see and stopping they will find.

Five miles or more, from where began the flight,
Along the summit of a woody hight,
Sir Maxey reins his courser to the ground,
And far and near for Rodney looks around.

As some dark cloud that spurns the rising gale,
Athwart it rolls and deepens in the vale,
Pours loud alarm upon the plains below;
Where, in midfield, stands the deserted plow,
And tall dread-breathing forests timid grow;
So seemed the surging courser as he trode,

With bois'trous hoof, to plunge along the road.

Now plodding near along the deep wood-side,
The expert of the wilds, Sir Maxey spied.
A brace of fowls and bleeding doe are strung
His rifle on and o'er his shoulder swung.
Homewards he strides anticipating toast,
Stewed fowl abundant, and savory roast.
"Here! Rodney! Here!" Sir Maxey urgent cries,
The expert pausing, lifts his downward eyes;
Alarm is flashing in his master's face,
With looks inquiring now he mends his pace,
When thus Sir Maxey loud begins to cry:
"Fly for your life! for God's sake, Rodney, fly!
A tribe of Sacs are swarming on my rear
Dreadful to see, but dreadful more to hear!
They'll scalp us all and burn the town I fear."
Towards the town the Champion lifts his eyes,
And on his master fixing, thus replies:
"No! let us meet them; hold your further flight,
Retreat's in order ne'er *before* a fight.
To fly will but reduce our wonted strength,
And make resistance feebler, and at length
Expose our village to the storming foe;

Who, if repulsed, will reinforcements show.
Lead not an enemy our helpless homes to know."
As some loud boar who hears his baying foes,
Upon his sedgy realms begin to close,
oaning rage flies from his hidings dense,
And throws his lordly strength on the defense;
So Rodney, from his cov'ring in the wood,
Flew to the breach, and waiting, *firmly* stood.
Straight he beheld the warriors close at hand,
Him they behold, his movements understand,
Wheel from his rifle, and their flight renew,
All, save two mightiest, to their man pursue.
These now dismounted, turn their ponies loose
And in the woods their vantage places choose,
Peer thro' the thick boughs with a stealthy eye,
Till at his mark one lets an arrow fly.
Thro' flinching branches rings the feathered harm,
And strikes its painful barb into his arm.
E'en as some bear whom crouching hunters wound,
Tears at the pain, and rages o'er the ground,
Till in the copse the hidden foe he spies,
And on his covert fierce as fury flies;
So Rodney, when the flinty stroke he feels,
The shaft plucks out, and from his cover wheels;
Rages defiant thro' the sounding wood,
Till near the wary foe his steps intrude.
Quick as some stag, when horns and hounds assail
His secret lair within the leafy vale;
The pluming champion springs upon his feet;
His and bold Rodney's eyes defiant meet.
Loud as two bulls that roar upon the plain,

Plunge on each others frothy sides amain,
Till wasted strength their foaming rage prevent,
The dread combatants groan with dire intent.

Each dreads the onset for the glare of death
Warms his foe's eyes, and fury wings his breath.
The chief's arm ne'er by wilds nor dangers swerved,

And Rodney's by successive hardships nerved,
With nervous haste their leathern girdles feel,
And on the gaze unsheath their deadly steel.
Each lifted hand its ghastly freight displays,
Each hurried glance the narrow field surveys;
With each, defiance can no farther go,
Unless it walk beyond a prostrate foe.
As two tall beeches shaken by the wind
Approach each other; now with heads inclined,
Now rush away with quick impetuous roar,
And now approach, inclining as before;
So bending to and fro the champions stand,
Till loud they rush together, hand-to-hand,
Rough as the surge when sounding billows meet
Between the schooners of an anchored fleet.
Each in his left hand holds the other's right,
And struggles o'er the ground in horrid plight,
Now on their knees, now bounding in the air,
And now half-stooped to earth, and groaning there.
Their lips all death-like on their teeth they clench
And grate defiance harsh at each long wrench,

That vainly strives the grasp to disengage,
And in the foe's heart plunge the steely edge.
The savage champion feels his waning strength
Give away, and yielding to his fears, at length
Pours forth three dreadful whoops of wild distress,
That start the lone ear of the wilderness.
An answer in the distance soon was heard,
And parting a dense thicket now appeared
A warrior fell, with cautious step and slow,
As when some cougar scents a covered foe.
New life to Rodney! Gracious Heaven save!
A doubled danger doubly nerves the brave!
He frees his knife with desp'rateness of strength,
And in the savage sheaths its deadly length;
And as he lifeless sinks with a loud groan,
Bold Rodney at the other heaves a stone.
Firm on his head the shrieking fragment flies,

The dying warrior rolls his painful eyes,
Sinks on the turf, that whitens with his brains,
And hugs the clod that drinks his flowing veins.

The dauntless hero of the woody waste,
To leave the scene of blood directs his haste;
With gun in hand, surveys his passage well,
And strides along the stream-divided dell;
Arrives in Saville ere the sun goes down;
Explains his wounds, and makes his combat known.
With tongues of praise the village meets her slave,

The women soothing, cheering him, the brave.

No strength has courage, to the fears disguise
In downcast glances of his serious eyes.
The horrid brake conceals the skulky foe,
And o'er him darkness falleth like a mantle low.
"Ah! Sad mistake!" the fathers of the town
In painful concert mutter up and down
The mournful streets; "Ah me! a fatal freak!
When wisdom yields to folly, valor's weak.
Ah, indiscretion! parent of all woe,
That causeth peace to rouse a crouching foe!
The sober blacksmith threw his hammer down,
And wiped the great drops from a sooty frown,
His anvil mounted, and with words of steel
Went on to utter what his heart did feel.
And as the sun sank in the hills' embrace,
His sad rays streaming in old Joseph's face,
That vacant looked, a picture made of dread,
That many strong hearts trembled as they read.
And Gabriel Grimes, the 'Squire, 'mong his books
Sat drown'd, assaying in his serious looks,
To trace a legal thicket on his gaze,
That showed no exit and no ent'ring ways.

"What? Ho!" Sir Maxey shouts with martial air,
"Before a struggle yield not to despair.
For these discretions valor makes amends,

We hold the means, but Providence the ends.
Fly to your arms, and set a heavy guard,
And coolness keep for strategy prepared.
Have wives and children shut in doors till morn,
And then will danger of his locks be shorn."

The honest cotters hear him with a sigh,
And glance around them with a doubtful eye;
Proceed toward the village church and stand
In dread suspense, a hopeless little band.
Now darkness lowers like a gloomy pall,
The muffled drum proclaims a solemn call,
And lights blown out reposeless courage waits
The signal of the sentry at the gates.
In converse low, the fathers watch in arms,
For night's familiar sounds now seem alarms.
The deep low baying of unusual curs,
Discloses restlessness not wholly theirs,
For honest dogs that stealthiness abhor,
Which doth conceal the steps of savage war.
Hark! List! a war-whoop starts the dismal fen!
A moment lingers, and is heard again.
Hope stops her flight, conjectures disappear,
Attack is certain, and is crouching near.
With noiseless tread the sylvan warrior steals,
(Him darkness in her mantle's folds conceals,)
Beneath the very cabin's walls, unseen,
And yet may pass the peering watch between.

When Heav'n responsive to his sally cries,
Will hideous grow, and shut her sickened eyes,
And from the pitchy womb of darkness born,
Red massacre behold the mournful morn.
Ah! now must Courage meet the unsheathed test
That makes stern manhood tremble in his breast.
Escape hath shut her paths upon his eye
And leaves him doomed to conquer or to die.

In age's low'ring look and muffled speech,
The young see trouble, and with sobs beseech
An explanation at the lips which hold
The dreadful secret that cannot be told.
Childhood avoids the wand of magic sleep;
Forgetfulness assays in vain to steep
His wakeful senses in her drowsy dews;
Close on composure's heels alarm pursues.
In solemn council lean the village sires,
Where hope's last smold'ring ember-glow expires;
Sir Maxey's indiscretions yet deplore,
And thus in concert sad their minds explore:
"Our ammunition most in hunting spent,
Our numbers scattered and resistance bent,
To send to Dearborn yet for aid remains
The only prospect that our reason gains,
That rises hopeful from disaster's plains.
The troops perhaps, by timely warning may,
In mounted march, rescue the sinking day.

But, who will go? Who'll dare these twenty miles,
Of forest peril, night and savage wiles?
Who'll bear the news, when he on foot must go,
For not a horse can 'scape the wary foe!"

The young and valiant called upon to choose
The way to glory or her hights refuse,
In vacant looks this truth leave manifest,
The glory-fires warm another's breast.
Then, as a hunter calls his faithful dog,
To dare the treach'rous sands and cross some bog,
Sir Maxey to his bleeding servant cries:
"Say, Rodney, can't you fly to Dearborn? Rise,
Your rifle take, be quick! look sharp! be gone!
Let what you do be well and quickly done."

As some firm rock that brawling floods oppose,
In all their wanton rage, Rodney arose,
Disgust red kindling in his manly face,

Looked on the lords of his unhappy race,
And spoke: "My masters, such your titles are,
Let all irreverence from my thoughts be far;
But I've till now a silent list'ner been,
And have your timid operations seen.
And now I ask, with but a servant's claim
To audience, and in a servant's name,
I ask, with what do brave men guard their wives,
And homes, and children, but with their *own* lives?

With all your bosoms cherish as their own,
With all they know, and all they've ever known,
Exposed to danger, sueing you for aid,
I ask, why have you this evasion made?
If I, an alien to your house and hearth,
The ignoble sharer of a slavish birth,
Am called to take your parts, be *well* apprised,
Your conduct is but cowardice disguised.
Had I a single treasure to me dear,
A single home joy bright, or, even were
I owner of my life, my arm I'd bare,
And thrust my fingers into peril's hair.
But none of these, and not a cheer within
My darkened breast, what may I hope to win?
Naught but the praise of mere obedience,
The fame of dogs! Nay! ere I journey hence,
Bring down command to tent with kind request,
Own me a man, and trust a manly breast.
For be assured, although your slave am I,
He will not cower, who will dare to die;
He sees no terror in menace's eye.
The gaping wounds I for my master wear,
Already warn me that I unrewarded bear."

Now, Rodney ended, and a mute despair
Fell on his hearers, for he breathed an air,
So foreign to their knowledge of a slave,
With liberty so audaciously brave;

That with the tameness of stupidity,
They on their bosoms leaned their chins, to see
Weak folly tamper with a lion; when
Sir Maxey turned away, and never spoke again.
In hope's wide fields there was no further day,
And now their only star had passed away.
As when beseiging cloud surround the hills,
Whose troubled bosom night with terror fills,
Rude shepherds tremble, in their darkened tent,
To hear the mountains wail and woods lament;
Till lo! upon the brim of vision far
Appears the joyous-beaming morning star;
So quaked these townsmen of St. Vincennes' wood,
Till in their midst fair Dora Maxey stood,
A ray of hope to all their bosoms dear,
A day-break in their cloud-gloom'd land of fear.
So young and gentle, so serenely wild,
At once a heroine and a lovely child!
The band dispersing with her conqu'ring eyes,
In daring tones to Rodney she replies:
"Brave servant, thou hast nobly said and true,
Let valor wear his scars and glory too,
But know that woman by her jealous lords
Unhindered, in her great heart e'er awards
To stalwart manhood, love, esteem and praise,
And glories most in his most daring ways.
By caste's frail grants let those win hearts who can,

What woman *loves* is manliness in man.
Now she is here, for *her* thy life expose,
And nobler years will her rewards disclose.
The time now wings this way, when Gratitude
Shall clasp thee to her bosom, and the good
And great, and brave of all the valiant earth
Will *own*, nay more, delight to own thy worth.
To Dearborn then and spread the dreadful news,
While danger's hights more timid souls refuse."

Now Rodney bow'd his face towards the ground,
Until his bosom this expression found:
"The humble subject of thy will I stand,
For thy request to me is a command,
The which to disobey's the coward's task,
Mine is to *do*, fair one, and yours to ask.

Now Dora's lilly-touch with sweetest haste,
Her father's weapons on his servant placed,
And thus the fortunes of the hour decides;
For he, with gun in hand and nimble strides,
The speechless groups of villagers divides,
With cougar caution slowly out proceeds,
But faster goes as further he recedes,
Till sent'nels past, deep in the howling night
His footsteps sink, and he is out of sight.

While still suspense with throbbing int'rest waits,
And slow-speeched dolour instances relates

Of grisly dangers conquered by the fates;
Of savage bands, when border strength was small,
Beat back from many a forest-cabin's wall,
Of women moulding as their husbands fired,
And children watching where the foe retired;
Fair Dora leaning on her elbow, sate
Within her window, o'er the village gate
That eastward looked towards Dearborn, and prayed
That Rodney's flight in no mishap be stayed.

The Fair Captive

The idle winds at dawn that strayed
Thro' wavy depths of joyous shade,
The early chirp of breeze-swung boughs,
The carol of the mountain brows,
The far off brawl of farms that broke
The drowsy silence of the morn,
And eager baying which awoke
Responsive to the flying horn,
In covert near, or echoing dell,
On Rodney's ear like omens fell;
For troubled Dearborn he had found
In need of all his garrison;
And now for Saville sadly bound
His pensive footsteps wander'd on.

Wild, strangely broken landscapes lay
Along his solitary way.
Soft gazing thro' the morning gray,
To right and left against the sky,
The border hills were stacked on high;
And as upon his eye they rose,
And shook their forests from repose,
Their brighter aspect on they drew,
A sober wear of filmy blue,

Like time's remotest visionary hue.

But Courage can no longer lie
With folded arms, when on his eye
There springs an opportunity.
Tho' beaten oft upon his walls,
And often tho' his banner falls,
Whene'er the day a breach supplies,
True Courage from defeat will rise,
And to renew the conflict flies.

Now in the lonely glen, or far
Amid the rocks whose shoulders bar
The toiling footsteps of young light,
Wild Rodney turns a nimbler flight.
No mountain stag, when clam'rous horns,
Him of the rousing danger warns,
Hath ever quicker brushed the dew,
Or fleeter leapt the deep shades thro',
Than Rodney fled with his sad tale
To 'larm the cotters in the vale.
His face with apprehension pale,
To many a woodman's open door,
The signal of disaster bore.

With gestures wild, to arms he called,
With words of war their hearts appalled,
And as the stout bands gathered;
He, warning others, flew ahead.

The settler on the doorsill rude
Of his poor forest-home, firm stood,
And as the news more wild would run,
He felt the triggers of his gun.
And glancing thro' the forests wide
To some near neighbor's 'gan to stride.
Thus Rodney from the forests drew
To meet the battle—not a few.
And as the corn-fields raised a shout,
And hills and valleys emptied out,
Bold hearts, that would the rescue try,
The hurried glance of many an eye;
The ceaseless pacing to and fro
Of those who waited; and the slow
And guarded accent of each tongue
That marked the speakers, them among,
Disclosed how thick that Peril hung
Her storm-swelled billows in the sky,
And troubled Peace's canopy.

The vale fermenting, Rodney left,
As lion-wild of young bereft;
And tho' the wasty forests wheeled
A speed that would have shamed the steeled
And wildest travel of the horse,
That snuffs up strength and leads the course.
By distant lodge and lone abode,
Where not a rudest fence, nor road,

A mark of civilization made
Within the vast primeval shade,
Untiring as the wind he strode.
Miles off a weary hill upon,
His early footsteps met the sun.
His eyes as earnest as the streaks
Of light that dashed along the peaks
In living crimson; far away
The nook sequestered did survey,
'Mid which his fated Saville lay.

A faint smoke rose, and slowly curled
In pensive wreaths against the sky,
And drifting farther off on high,
Like visions of the glory-world;
Hung sadly on the distant shore
Of indistinctness; then passed o'er,
Now dimly seen, now seen no more.
What apprehensions thrilled him now!
What dread conjectures clenched his brow
Had Saville just from calm repose
Awakened? Or had pluming foes
Her cheerful homes in ashes lain,
And heaped her sacred hearths with slain?
The dilatory smoke seem'd born
Of blazing plenty's stirring morn,
Or rolling from a famished fire,
That had in its devouring ire

Licked up all life that near it lay,
And turned to eat itself away.
Down from the hights his way along,
From rock to rock, till lost among
The lofty woods that bowed and sighed,
He turned with yet untiring stride;
And from the intervening vale,
Emerged and stood aghast and pale.

Lo! all his hopes had crumbled to the dust;
Saville had fallen in the direful fight;
And from devouring Ruin's fire-jaws thrust
Her poor remains, disgorged by sickened night
In morning's lap, yet steamed an ember-smould'ring sight.
Coal heaps where homes once stood, and bodies charred,
Of innocence and beauty in the heaps;
Scalped heads from love's keen knowledge even barred,
By savage battle's hands; and little steeps,
Where wound the village paths to field or wood,
Made red and slippery with kindred blood,
Were sights that filled the hero's saddened eyes;
The tributes gathered by hostilities.
Ah! how destruction's devastating hand
There fell upon delights! How his eyes scanned
With gorgon glee, the ghastly path he made
Thro' Peace's bow'rs within the western shade!
And like a jackal at the lion's side,
There Folly laughed to see her fallen pride.

Lo! now the Champion bends his daring brow,
And thro' the ruins plods pond'ringly slow;
A sob suppresses, sighing, "Me! ah, me!
O, Dora! fairest Dora! where is she?"
A low'ring cloud encamps around his soul,
And sorrow's big rain down his troubled cheek doth roll.

A tiny heel-print leaving, lo! he spies,
In which there here and there a torn spray lies;
A flash of joy light'nings in his eyes.

The way it moves, with breathing hushed he views,
And eager as a rolling flood, pursues.
Thro' dense shades leaning, now he threads along,
He gains commanding hills, high woods among.
With fearless steps, divides the lowly vale,
And like a mountain hart, the rocks beyond doth scale.

Of how he sped for eager miles away;
How strange scenes filled the melancholy day,
Of how the rustle of some waste-fed herd,
How plantive woods that piped and chirped and stirred;
Or how the distant cat'ract's pensive moan
Alarmed or moved him, cannot here be shown;
But on in wild pursuit he ponders still,
And stands at sundown, on an oak-brow'd hill,
When solemn night comes on with noiseless tread,
And o'er the landscape doth her rayless mantle spread.

Not many paces had the night come on

Blund'ring with sable steps, when still, upon
A log sat Rodney in despondent mood;
When, lo! a light approached him in the wood.
"What!" arising, cries he, in an undertone,
"Is this which haunts me in these wilds alone?"
And quick aside he noiselessly steals,
To where a denser shade his halt conceals;
When two old women of the skulky bands,
Mope by with pots of water in their hands.
Torches they bear, upon their way to shine,
In oil steeped, and riven from the pine.
He marks their movements with an eager eye,
Their way pursues, and waits discovery.
So when some mastiff thro' the sleeping folds,
A stranger passing, loiteringly, beholds,
He waiting lies, or follows crouching low,
The errand of the visitor to know;
When, if in thieving he his hands invest,
A roaring chastisement will him arrest.

Now where beyond the vale a cliff ascends,
Around whose base an unknown river bends,
A smoking camp the peering watcher spies,
And warlike satisfaction lights his eyes.
Beneath the stooping boughs he can behold
The busy squaws swarm'd round by warriors bold.
Then in the rocks, a score of yards away,
He like a crouching lion eyes his prey.

"Oh, Heav'n!" he gasps, and turns his painful eyes
From where in hideous hands his Dora lies,
To raving lusts a fair and tender prize,
Fair as a moon that o'er the night's face steals,
And gaping rocks and grizly wastes reveals,
The sweet and patient face of Dora shone
Upon these scourges of the wilds unknown.
The rabble now in high confusion runs,
Their knives the warriors grapple, now their guns.
Claim the fair triumph ere the game decides,
While shouting might the opposing voice derides.
Soon other methods they to conquest choose,
This one or that the tiny captive woos
With wild expressions of languishing love,
Like demons longing for the light above.
With heated eyes they stare into her face,
Drag her soft bosom in a rough embrace;
Their beads display, their painted head-gear show;
Like satyrs gibber, and like monsters blow.
Sweet as the vespers of some plaintive stream,
Or as the sounds in a mid-summer's dream,
Dora lisps something with her fair hands clasped,
When, "Ah, my God, she prays!" wild Rodney gasped.
The camp-fires glare upon her lifted hands,
And on her wrists disclose the bloody bands.
When, in the night, the hero thrusts his form,
Fierce as the lightning-arm that strikes the storm.

A stalwart warrior hands the pleading maid,
And drags her roughly thro' the darkling shade,

While to her tender remonstrance replies
A monster's scowl, and laughter mocks her cries.
The fiery watcher scans the dark field o'er,
And finds a smooth way straight his feet before.
Now all his strength he in his poised arm flings,
The impatient moment checks its onward wings;
Till like an eagle dropping from the skies,
Right on the howling band the swift avenger flies.

A flash of steely lightning from his hand,
Strikes down the groaning leader of the band;
Divides his startled comrades, and again
Descending, leaves poor Dora's captor slain.
Her, seizing then within a strong embrace,
Out in the dark he wheels his flying face;
His victims leaves to struggle with surprise,
And like a phantom thro' the forest flies.
She, brave as steel, against his bosom lies;
Gasps, "Rodney, is it you, or but a dream!
Oh, have you come! Oh, are things what they seem?"
He speaks not, but, with stalwart tenderness
Her swelling bosom firm on his doth press.
Leaps like a stag that flees the coming hound,
And like a whirlwind rustles o'er the ground.
Her locks swim in dishevelled wildness o'er
His shoulders, streaming to his waist or more;

While on and on, strong as a rolling flood,
His sweeping footsteps part the silent wood.
Now low beneath the list'ning boughs he leant,
Now thro' the tow'ring upland swifter bent,
And on a hill, where in her gentler sway,
The open sky lent vision one dim ray,
He pausing stood, to cast a look around,
And catch, if possible, some warning sound.
But all was still; the wide world was asleep,
Save that a waking night-wind there did creep.
Then Dora, like a heroine fair and true,
Cried, "Rodney! Rodney! Ah, I know 'tis you."

"Yes, Dora," lisps the Champion, and applies
His bloody knife to loose her painful ties;
When, like a bird that mounts on airy wing,
To dash into the light of joyous spring,
She rose, she fluttered to his strong embrace,
With streams of joy pouring down her upturned face.
Heaven might envy such a scene as this,
Since angels ken no more of perfect bliss
Than, when disaster and a direful day
Conspire to lead a fair young life away
In captive chains, to red-eyed lusts a prey,
Is felt by him whose fearless hand rescues,
Tho' howling danger on his devious path pursues.

Miles further on the twain in converse stand,
Where depth on depth of rayless wastes expand;

Together lean, and on their lone way peer,
Listen, to catch night's voices; but hear
Their hearts leap only, and the footfalls weird,
That round the anxious lonely heart are always beating heard.
From gaping wounds much Rodney's strength has flown;
Against a tree he sets his rifle down,
Submits to Nature's soft compelling sway,
And there concludes to bide returning day.
His blanket winds his manly form around,
And spreads his weary length along the ground.
"Here, Dora," then he speaks, "rest on my arm,
My life shall stretch between you and all harm;
Your frail and much worn strength some rest must have,
Or you'll escape the foe to find a grave."

No word speaks Dora, but her timid eyes
Survey the spot where her defender lies;
Then as a lamb when prowling wolves appear,
The horned defender of the folds will near,
She 'proaches Rodney; stands in trustful mood
And looks around her in the dismal wood.
Reluctant now, and innocently shy,

She kneels upon her turfy couch close by,
Her hands extend, so delicately white,
In earnest prayer unto the God of Night,
In grace Divine upon her to descend,
And o'er her guardian to in gentle mercy bend.

Then in his bosom nestles with deep sighs
That bring great drops of sadness to his eyes.
"Oh sleep, descend, and seal thy lovely sight!"
Said Rodney in his heart; "no harm this night
Can thee befall. And when the op'ning day
Shall spread her gentler guidance on our way,
My life shall guard the way before thy feet;
Tho' dangers thronging thick, await us there to meet."

The bending heavens drop a tear and sigh,
Old forest sent'nels spread their shelter nigh,
And night winds burthened with their heavy dews,
Strip off their chillness, and their soft sounds use,
While in deep musings sits the pensive hour
And fills composure's urn in slumber's quiet bower.
Robing the hills in light and beauty, now
A late moon hangs upon yon mountain's brow,
Looks stilly on the world's round sleeping face,
Then veiled in silver clouds withdraws with queenly grace.
Now Dora wakes from strange and fitful dreams,
The brightest rival of the bright moon's beams.
Soft light between the parting branches steals,
And Rodney's stern, still, manly brow reveals.
In him who slumbers, one can better read
The master passions and the thoughts which lead;
For, then the face, obedient to no call
Of shrewd deceit, shows nothing false at all;
But on the features silent truth doth write

Her plainest letters, in their plainest light.
Thus, sighing, looked the fair young frontier maid
Into the sleeper's open face, and said:

"What deep marks there hath hardship's plow-share laid?
Reserve how manly there! What self-control!
What resolution! Ah a man of soul!"
Then, as some bird that hails the bloom-crowned spring,
O'er sunny meadows spreads her wayward wing,
And joyous flits where all the woodlands sing;
Dora, as wayward, lifts her lovely mouth,
Sweet as the dewy blossoms of the South;
On Rodney's forehead parts the tangled hair,
And gently leaves affection's impress there.
He wakes; and straightway Dora whispers: "Look
How yonder moon lights up this lonely nook
With silver glory! Could I but forget
Dear Saville, and the scenes that haunt me yet,
Rapt fancy here would build a wild retreat,
And gladly linger in her forest seat."
Then Rodney, rising: "Day is almost here,
For now the Seven Stars do disappear;
So, think not, Dora, o'er the past to brood,
For loneliness abhors a theme of blood;
The day may o'er your sorrows brightness fling;
The saddest Winter hath a joyous Spring.
Hope on, for this sweet dream I had to-night:
I stood high on a farm-surrounded hight,

Where fruitful hills rose round the even view,
Not indistinct, but robed in charming blue.
There, sober herds in peaceful order strayed,
And tinkling folds enliven'd the evening shade.
Love's pensive reed wound the fair vales along,
Or sauntered leisurely his flocks among.
Now I reclining on my elbow leant,
To sweet winds list'ning as they came and went,
And tuned their many stringed pleasurement;
When, o'er me bending, ere I saw from where,
An angel stood in golden waves of hair
Half drowned. Regarding me with care, she drew
Nearer, kissed my forehead, and upward flew."

Then spake the angel of the hero's dream:
"Surely some happy token that doth seem,
And, could we but unveil the mystery,
And now discover the vast yet to be,
Some future bliss we both in it might see."
And with evasive sweetness now she turns
To where the mournful waste, her Saville's ashes urns.

Much she relates, and Rodney sorrowing hears,
Sometimes with groans responsive, sometimes tears.
The waiting town in deep suspense she shows,
While brake and fen are howling with her foes.
With heavy countenance and long drawn sighs,
Danger asserts her reign in valor's eyes;

The women weep, and pray, and tear their hair,
And raise a storm of turbulent despair.
Children and women now are barred in doors,
Without, the heavy footed tumult roars,
And loud is heard the bloody-handed fray.
The townsmen struggle, but are swept away.
Out in the storm the screaming children fly,
And frantic mothers follow where they fly,
But this on Rodney's soul doth saddest stay
Dora is dragged a captive in the wilds away.

Fair Dora ended here, and Rodney rose,
Walked from the boughs that did their rest enclose,
And said: "Let's journey, yonder comes the morn;
See! how the mountains laugh the vanquished night to scorn!
And hand in hand they meet the bright-eyed day,
As on to Dearborn Rodney leads his lovely prize away.

Fort Dearborn

Fort Dearborn is a strong and goodly place,
And o'er the frontier looks with valiant face
To greet the hostile tread of savage harm,
With tongue of thunder and an iron arm.
Far up he stands, on a commanding ground,
With grizly turrets rising high around:
Block houses rude protect the outer posts,
Where pass the sentries quick before the camping hosts.

Here, erst, as eagle drives the trembling dove
O'er meadows broad, to shelt'ring cliffs above;
Proud Black Hawk rose, stern monarch of the wood,
The red Napoleon of Solitude,
And drove young civilization from the West,
To fly and hover in loud Dearborn's breast;
Till peace returning, with a gentle hand,
Beckoned her forth again to plant the flow'ry land.

Long since the Nation's battle-arm had cleared
Her skirts of border outrages; and reared
By daring hands, the settler's cabin stood,
By every stream and in the mighty wood;
Since labor found in ease's arms repose—
This strong avenger of his race arose;
And vindicating, or for woe or weal

The red-man's homes, unsheathed the battle steel,
And made the border throat, alas! his bloody logic feel.

He saw neath mammon's desecrating tread,
The turf-green dwellings of the sacred dead.
The forest sachem, and the honored sire,
No more, within their lofty homes, awoke the fire
Of burning council in the patriot breast;
His sun sunk now forever on the wigwam-smoking West.
His leaping streams with cascade sadness mourned,

His fleet canoe was from its moorings turned,
His squaws and children bade their fields adieu,
To starving on their tearful way pursue;
And bloody-armed aggression followed where they flew.
Oh! who can then approach the chieftain's shade,
With ought but honor, e'en tho' he was made
To tear his heart from ev'ry tend'rer tie,
And to his loved ones with an arm of hostile succor fly?
Great hero, peace! Thou and thy thousand braves,
Too weak to stand, too proud to e'er be slaves,
On valor's lips, shall to the list'ning years
Be told: and urned in woman's love and tears,
Thy name to Time's remote end carried down,
Shall treasured be and claimed, by high Renown.

As some fierce comet rises in the West,
With locks of flame—and in deep crimson drest—
Swims ominously up a troubled sky,

With fury stationed in his fiery eye;
While panting superstition drops a tear,
Prophetic looks, and thinks Time's end is near;
So, in Migration's pathway thou didst rise,
The flaming terror of the border skies,
And so aggression looked on thee with fearful eyes.

Young morn descending from her Eastern tour,
Now on the mountains chased a panting show'r;
The vap'rous slumbers of the valleys broke,
And to the waking fields a sweet breath'd greeting spoke.
On wings of song, enliv'ning cheer went round,
O'er sad-voiced woods by Autumn suns embrowned,
And o'er farm-studded vales, with here and there
An orchard neat, that crowned some rustic's care,
And friendly cot, beside the hillside stream,
The rude ideal of his glory dream.
Then, in a gate that looked from Dearborn West,
Sir Maxey stood, and thus his soul exprest:
"My Dora! Oh, my Dora! Where is she?

Torn from my care, oh, saints, how can it be!
To pine away in desert wastes and die,
Or feed the savage lusts that on her breast may lie.
My only Dora! Would I ne'er had been;
Or that I never had my angel seen!
Oh, my life's flower, doomed to droop and faint,
Where ling'ring exile mocks thy lone complaint!
Bereavement's hand poured out my grief to full,

And gave me sorrow from a ghastly skull;
When from my side, that one who shared my cares,
The burden-bearer of my weighty years—
Was borne away, my home to light no more!
E'en then Hope whispered of a sainted shore.
But tongueless sits Despair, dark-plumed with dole,
And strikes her painful beak into my soul!
When something to my sad heart seems to say,
"'Thy Dora pines in desert wilds away.'"

Two captains who upon their steeds had sate,
And heard him thus lamenting in the gate;
Now putting spurs, together eager cry:
"Withhold thy woeful 'plaint, where chivalry
Will test his strength. Say to us, aye, oh Sire,
And we will rescue Dora ere the day expires."

"Aye," cries Sir Maxey, "hear a father's vows;
Who rescues Dora, hath her for a spouse,
And purse of gold besides. Now, Westward fly,
And haste thy search, for we have this surety,
Of him, the only one who scaped the foe,
Her captors on a Westward way did go."

Swift as the shadows of a flying cloud,
From Dearborn forth now rode the soldiers proud;
But ere their morn of glory had begun,

High in their brightest sky, appeared a brighter sun.
Rodney came leading Dora from a wood,
And in their presence like a vision stood.

Their steeds they reined, they made a martial bow;
On Rodney gazed, awed by his valiant brow;
Glanced then at Dora, and together sighed:
"Whose she shall be, the future must decide!"
But ere their admiration found a tongue,
She passed them by the village trees among.

"My life no more embraces pure delight,"
Sighs one, "With that fair maiden out of sight!"
The other echoes. "My life's shine is o'er,
If I must see that beauty rare no more!"
"But," then the other mourns, "her father vows,
That who rescues her hath her for a spouse!
When, if the valiant task hath now been done
By yon stern slave, our prospects darken neath an eclipsed sun."
"A slave contend," his friend indignant spoke,
"In love's fair lists, and wear a master's yoke!
A servant dog, a stalwart negro clown,
Unhorse a knight, the queen of love to crown?
Nay, thanks to Jove, the negro's proper sphere,
Is by him wilfully abandoned ne'er,
His longings suited to his station are;
For faithfulness he craves a master's care,

And craves no more; he stoops a bashful face
From azure looks, and love's white-arm'd embrace.
Born to be ruled, kind nature seals his breast
'Gainst Cupid's darts and Hymen's visions blest.
In him ambition's merest insolence,
And chivalry is brazen impudence."
"Between us then," the other aptly cries,
"The open list, of flow'ry conquest lies,
And let the god's to excellence award the prize."

Now, Dora turning from the perilous wild,
Ran to a waiting father's long embrace,
And kissed the streams of joy from his face.
Brave Dearborn shouted o'er the rescued child,
Till loud rejoicings from his iron throat,

Rolled o'er the wastes and shook the hills remote.
Round after round the cheering cannon rung,
Old Solitude for once had found a tongue,
And spoke responsive, her deep lone retreats among.
All day the eyes of pleasure sparkled bright,
Around the evening hearth the circling news gave light;
The hand of valor, beauty's fair hand shook,
And joy beamed forth in age's sober look.
The tragic fate of Saville hindered not,
So much was sorrow in their mirth forgot.

Lo! where yon gloomy walls ascend on high;
Whose dismal windows meet the passing eye,

Where Memphis rises in her steepled pride,
And gazes on fair Mississippi's tide,
Where Memphis, robed in glitt'ring wealth doth rise,
The boast of Tennessee, the pride of Southern skies.
Turn there thy foot, thou who hast wandered long
Thro' life's sad ways, and by the haunts of wrong;
Thou who hast heard of mammon hardened souls,
Who drank iniquity from brimming bowls,
Or who hast dreampt of Slavery's grinding car,
Mounted by Crime, and dragged by dogs of war;
Followed by Famine, whose skeleton hand
Compels submission from a trembling land;
While empty Ignorance's idiot smile,
The hard-gleaned tribute is, to custom vile:
Turn there thy foot, thou who hast heard or read
Of virtue, chained to lust's infamous bed;
Pause at the door! The keeper comes! I hear
His footsteps on the stony floor anear!
The slow key grates, bolts move, oppressed I feel,
The sullen prison opes its jaws of steel;
And in the Hell of Slavery aghast I reel.

Among the sable inmates now I wend
My way, and they in fervent aspect bend
Their faces in the dust, cry, "Massa!" "Lord!"

But their bright tearful eyes speak more than cry or word.
They kiss their haughty keeper's iron hand,
Pursue his way, or round him suppliant stand.

Ah! Christian, canst thou bear it? Turn thine eyes
To where yon sorrow burdened mother lies!
She upward looks, and wrings her anguish, see!
Say to her, "Woman, oh, what aileth thee?"
And thou shalt hear the tearful answer sad,
"Two children, once to cheer my life I had;
The one was three years old, a little girl,
Her brow was clustered o'er with many a curl,
Her eyes were bright, and blue as Summer's skies!
But oh, my sweet faced darling!" loud she cries,
"My babe! Dear Willie! Oh, my two-month's old!
Was from my bosom snatched away, by cold
And cruel hands—methinks I hear his cry—
To pine without a mother's care and die!
Behold that mother, Christian, she is hushed
By yon stern keeper's glance, e'en though her soul is crushed.
And yonder see hoar age from friendship torn,
And from the goodly scenes where he was born!
Burdened with grief, he leans toward the grave,
And drags his chains, a poor unpitied slave.

This is the slave pen, reader, this the place
Where boasting Slav'ry drives the sable race,
To wait, as trembling sheep the slaughter wait,
Their buyer's entrance at yon iron gate.
Here tender hands of tearful remonstrance,
Entreating age's humble upward glance,

The sudden out-bursts of the grief torn heart,
The infant's 'plaint, from parent arms apart,
The maniac's wail and gaunt-eyed hunger's sigh,
That e'en doth bring a tear in Heaven's eye,
Cannot in man's cold heart, awake dead sympathy.

Ah, Tennessee, hast thou a Hermitage,
Where dwel'st a laurelled hero and a sage?

Great sage! Proud leader of the daring band,
Who loosed red havoc from the battle hand
On Blount's poor fort, till hardy sea-worn tars,
With crime acquainted, and athirst for wars,
Withdrew, their heads hung, from the scenes of blood,
Or o'er the mangled inmates weeping stood!
Let Silence rest her hand upon thy mouth,
And cease thy boasts, Oh, vain Chivalric South!
Say to thy mem'ry, "Ah, lead me not back
In yon deep ghostly past, with visions black!"
Thou may'st forget that from their brake-bound seat,
As free, true hearts, as e'er to freedom beat,
Were dragged in chains, fastened by Slavery's laws,
Or chased by bloodhounds, from whose gaping jaws,
Dropped human gore, to stain the sacred soil
That bloomed and grew beneath the hand of toil.
'Thou may'st forget, in a repentant soul,
The wigwams of the wasted Seminole;
And in the world's great temple, at the shrine
Of patriotism, kneel neath hands divine.

Lo! where yon whirling to and fro
Of men in business tide; doth so
Intoxicate with eagerness;
And in the eddy of voices hear,
The shrill cry of the auctioneer!
"Agoing! going!" rises clear.
While crowds of anxious list'ners press,
And doubt and gaze, and sigh and guess;
Shrewd speculation, in the face
Of business looks: his quick eyes trace
The way of vantage, till he make
A fortune, or a fortune break.
Suspense's trembling speech is heard,
For now the crier, word by word,
Sinks lower, lower, "going, gone,"
The bargain 's clasped, the work is done;
And now he calls another one.
There, rising as the wave-dashed rock,

Firm in his tow'ring scorn;
There, standing on the buyer's block,
See that sad form, but not forlorn.
In other climes was he not born?
Yes, where yon Western bowers spread
Their green luxuriance o'er the head
Of bare-armed labor, and the sound
of rural sports, the long year round,
Is heard on care's enlivened way;

He once hath known a brighter day.
There where young industry's strong arms
Hath in the forests hewn down farms,
And in the vale his pastures spread,
And by the waters clean flocks fed;
Full harvests reaped upon the hills,
And in the valleys built his mills;
There, once he mingled, true and brave,
A home-guard loved, and faithful slave.
'Tis Saville's Rodney, Dora's friend,
A faithful servant to the end.
And do you ask why he is sold?
I answer, then you shall behold.

There is a famous spring by Dearborn's walls,
Whose rush bound wand'ring to the heart recalls,
Of frontier daring, olden memories,
That oft bring brightness, oft tears to the eyes.
Here erst the Sachem, in his plumy pride,
Beheld his clans reposing at his side,
When on the tongue of forest councils burned
The words of war, or, when, in peace returned
From weary hunting grounds, they cheerful lay,
To watch the painted face of dying day.
Here civilization met his savage foe,
And with an arm of lightning laid him low,
And on the open hights of triumph stood,
Clasping this lucent treasure of the wood.

Here now the peaceful villagers repair,
To soothe the burdened ear of cumb'rous care.
Lo! yonder lab'rer, from his field comes by,
And nears with quick'ning steps and brightened eye.
Here trysting whispers linger in the shade,
Where rustic courtship clasps his bashful maid,
And sober converse, to the scene endeared,
Tarries till vespers soft are in the village heard.
Hail thou best blessing of the varied train,
That cheers life's journey thro' earth's weary plain!
Nectar for gods, and bright wines for the king,
But draughts for lab'rers from the running spring.

Now Dora stood at this ancestral spot,
And list'ning to the waters sing, forgot
That she was waiting for her running over pot.
Loud jovial labor in the field was done,
And sounds of mellow night-fall had begun,
The swallow told her stories in the eaves,
The groaning wain creaked home beneath its sheaves,
The swain garrulous in his empty weal,
Debated with the hills, till sudden wheel
Of rooky clamor from the elms, made
His hair stand up, till he had crossed the shade.
The shrill cock blew, the hillside barn behind;
And crow belated, asks the sent'nel wind,
Which way was nearest to his roosting mates.
The reaper homeward sang thro' slamming gates,

And o'er the sheep-cote woods a moon hung pale,
Like some lone shepherdess that hears a lover's tale.
Now Dora wond'ring what the waters said,
Leaned o'er the rocks and lingered in the shade,
Till Rodney, standing at her elbow, spake:
"You to obey, this only chance I take,
Now to my aching heart the secret ope;
May I to hear some pleasant tidings hope?"
Then Dora answered, "Oh! my faithful slave,
In my distresses well didst thou behave.

The life of me, and of my father too,
Are to thy manly, brave exertions due;
But thou hast kindled, by thy interest,
The fires of jealousy in many a breast.
Hence, thou art sold. The two commanders here
Have followed thee with bitterness severe,
Till for thy safety, father has thee sold,
Away to Memphis, Tennessee, I'm told.
But Rodney, bear it! In God's strength be bold!"

In the House of the Aylors

Where Summer crowns with orange blooms
The land of pines and cypress glooms;
We wander forth by field and lane,
In woody shades with plaintive strain.
Ye lonely bayous catch the sound!
Ye languid fen-brakes pass it round;
Ye pensive hills your silence break,
And let the mournful echo wake!
Of errant Pride's chivalric deeds,
Of frowning Caste's unholy creeds,
And their worse, sin-begotten heir,
Black Slavery, a lay I bring,
And of *her* painted crimes dare sing.

When Satan, hurled down from the skies,
O'er this terrene his fallen eyes
In search of ruin hotly cast,
Hell-bound, but harm-bent to the last;
Those shores of ours, where Mexic's Sea
Holds watch with the Atlantic, he
Touched not in his tremendous flight;
For, stooping there, the sons of light
He spied encamped in battle form
Around a captive ocean storm,

From which his equinoctial bent,
Wheeled short, and further northward went.

Sweet land! conceived in chivalry,
Brought forth in wild adventure, reared
In conquest's arm, to rivalry
And old ambitions long endeared!
The fairest of thy sister train
And fairer than thy mother Spain,
Thou art of all the world a lone,
Lone beauty of the fragrant zone.

Thy sisters in their lurid North
Surpass in wealth but not in worth;
More native grace hast thou than they,
Less wrathful winds and winters gray.
Thou hast no somber-low'ring skies,
In which the white-winged tempest flies;
Where shiv'ring woods aloud bewail,
All riven by the angry gale,
Their cheerless, torn, and chilly state,
Like empty beggars at your gate.
But such thy distant sisters know,
Within their wintry wastes of snow,
And hills as speechless as the tomb,
And sullen plains of voiceless gloom.
But girdled in thy summer zone,
As a maid who waits her lover,
Or to meet him walks alone

Under twilight's dewy cover,
Thou dost come to meet each year,
Always smiling, never drear.
And can it be, that thou, this goodly land,
Could foster slavery with a jealous hand?
Yea, when less comely States had seen the stain,
Of crimson guilt upon their skirts too plain,
They shook the galling traffic from the clutch
Of commerce, and forbade her further such.
But thou, when banished Slavery left the North,
In wretchedness and shame, to wander forth,
A heartless strumpet, seeking e'en a shed;
Thou then did'st take her in and share thy bed!
And can'st thou wonder that thy hardened heart
Should make humanity's shoulders smart,
When to errantic crime thou wast a bride,
When Pagan barbarism wedded Roman pride?

Of him whose valor first inspired our strain,
A slave to Aylor bound we sing again.
The shady woodlands of his native West,

To him are not: in richer verdure drest,
A fairer aspect Florida presents,
But not more pleasure; that which most contents
A noble mind, the liberty to dare
And do, the man, he now no more can share.
To him what are luxurious verdure's sweets,
And cypress shades, and orange-bloom'd retreats;

When for once dear delights his heart now hopeless beats?
Lo! where yon hedge-bound fields beyond the way,
Wave on the view exuberently gay,
Exulting in their flow'ry excellence,
And clasping in their green embrace, a dense
Deep grove of sturdy pines whose solemn shade,
Has o'er delicious seats a curtain made;
There stood the Aylor house, when in its prime,
A brave old structure of that princely time,
When rank and title held unquestioned sway,
And humble worth to fam'ly pride gave way.
How often have I, turning to its bowers,
In dreams sat down and wasted pleasant hours.
How often traced its various changing scenes
Of blossom'd fields, bright lanes, and rolling greens!
This goodly mansion hath an olden fame,
And memories that urn full many a name
In honors bright and not a few in shame.
Here hoary tenants, who in turn await
Their scanty pensions at a master's gate;
These, and full many an ebon patriarch,
Of Afric's humble tribe, who wear the mark
Of bondage, tell in tales of cabin lore,
Sad things that run the eye with pity o'er.
Thus of the Aylor line we are informed:
"When erst colonial patriotism stormed
New England's early hights, and stretched the hand

Of burning eloquence o'er all the land;
And Puritanic piety, allured
By Siren Freedom to the wilds, endured

The long privations of the wilderness,
With all the unction of true holiness,
The Aylors mingled with the daring few,
Who in the tyrant's face the blade of battle drew.

With vict'ry flushed on fortune's swelling tide,
Young Aylor soon had won a lovely bride,
The fairest flower of New England's pride.
Ere long, embarked in love's light craft, they join
With oars of labor, and their hopes incline
To stem life's tide; to fortune's source explore,
And in the future near touch happiness' shore.
Soft are the winds that swell their first short sail,
And mild their skies, ne'er angered by a gale.
Glad waves arise to kiss their peaceful keel,
And from their prow bright silv'ry ripples steal,
New ambient hills their ravished vision thread,
New argent fields and tinkling valleys spread;
Love lends new relish as new scenes invite;
Hope points to others not yet on their sight,
And gently heaves the deep beneath their dove-like flight.
To them the world is one ovation grand,
Where fortune show'rs bright favors from her hand,
And fancy beckons to a blissful land.
Florida the inviting aspect shows,

And here full soon the Aylor mansion rose.
There, husbandry soon stooped to till the soil,
And ripened plenty filled the lap of toil.
Bright Spring on Winter's parting steps pursued,
With buds and flowers his ling'ring footprints strewed,
Her cornfields spread, and orchards in the dell,
And waited till the big rain's benediction fell.

Full, blue-eyed Summer, stately coming on,
With shouting harvests stood the hills upon;
The breath of wasting juices did inhale,
With bloomy cotton whitened in the vale,

Spread out the ripened cane along the steep,
And waving rice fields in the swamp did reap.

Then Autumn came, with sickle keen in hand,
And yellow sheaves beneath her arm; to stand
And with her mellow voice to fill the land.
The waning fields sank on the saddened view,
And melancholy hills were robed in blue.
Brown Autumn came, and at her solemn close,
The swarthy hands of labor found repose.
Then sports set in, and harmless games began,
And through the livelong snowless winter ran.
What cares had slaves to mar their peace with dole,
And shut the light of mirth out from the soul,
When life-long labor made them richer none—
When nothing earned was theirs when work was done?
What reasons they to look back with remorse,

When careful conduct made their state the worse
Or better none? Their lives were not their own;
Hence past and future were to them unknown.
Hard labor's respite came, and as it neared,
Their burdens lightened and their hearts were cheered.
Religion, work and pastime, all in turn,
They had; but art and science must not learn.
And yet, contentment these vast wants supplied,
And loaned the pleasures caste had them denied.
The mind that never grasped hypotheses,
Nor wandered in the maze of theories;
Nor toil'd thro' demonstrations intricate,
Nor groaned beneath old histories' vast weight,
Can best afford in other paths *well* known,
To seek for pleasures not so over grown
The last day's labor was a day of feast,
And toil-earned freedom for both slave and beast.
The groaning barns were filled from floor to eaves,
And all the barnyard stacked around with sheaves.
Then, when the last full load of ripened corn
Was gathered in, the master took his horn,

And mounted high upon the rounded pile,
Rode homewards, sounding, followed by a file
Of empty wagons; while a lusty band
Of slaves came shouting on at either hand.
The shorn fields sank forsaken on their view,
And as they nearer to the barnyard drew,

Slave cabins emptied out a roaring crowd,
And gabbling hillsides answered them aloud.
When shouts of triumph closed the boist'rous scene,
The master king, and mistress crowned a queen.
This edict then, thro' all *her* milder reign
Of hut-bound realms, awoke a glad refrain
In servitude's full heart. "Go waste the hours
As you may wish, good slaves; the time is yours
From now till blooming Spring shall come again,
And spread her painted sweets upon the plain."

They then set in with ev'ry setting sun,
And danced till they were tired of the fun.
Loud rang the fiddle on three strings or four,
But louder rang their feet upon the floor.
The music, started once, as well might cease,
For joy kept up the dance with lively ease.
Now all hands joined, their circling knew no bound,
Save that they paused to catch the music's sound;
And when caught, all hands joined around again,
They whirled away to overtake the strain.
Then, balanced all, they stood out pair and pair,
And trampled hugely down the flying air.
Thus on they strode till night's last watch had flown,
Or they had broke the smiling fiddler down;
Who, sweating like a hunter in the chase,
Dragged his bandanna o'er a hopeless face;
Sore puzzled, grinned, and chided, out of breath,

"Ah! darkies, will you dance a man to death?"

Long ran their joyance thro' the grateful years,
The slave as happy as his lord appears;

For then true guardian, the master deemed,
In all but rank his servants kindred seemed.
With him communing at the Paschal feast,
Where no distinctions met the humblest guest;
And with him at the nuptial altar kneeling,
His fervent prayer the holy union sealing;
He, round his dying couch, with sleepless care,
Life's comforts brought, and knew no pains to spare;
Leaned tearful o'er him till his latest breath,
And closed his faithful eyes to sleep the rest of death.
But Avarice, whose reign is rife with woe,
To earthly bliss the deepest venom'd foe,
In this proud mansion found a lurking place,
At first discovered as a youthful grace,
At last unveiling all her frightful face.
The air grew tainted from her baleful lungs,
And Discord there unloosed her howling tongues.
There Anger's raging thirst was slaked with blood
Drawn from the back of groaning Servitude.
From bad to worse the Aylor house went down;
In phrenzy's bowl adversities they drown,
Thro' halls of revel banished joys pursue,
Exhaust old pleasures, madly pine for new;
Chase wanton transports thro' the mazy dance,

And seek their wasted fortunes at the hand of chance.
Then feuds and murder hurry to the scene,
And fam'ly pride's dear bowers are there no longer green.
An orphan heir to violence and shame,
Now one lone Aylor, Mosher is his name,
Holds undisputed all his lawful claim.
The hand of love and beauty both he scorns,
With broken vows, his wanton rites adorns,
And in his mansion's every nook and hall,
With open lewdness holds high carnival.

This brief narration, with its changes fraught,
Hath us once more to meet with Rodney brought.
The cabin dance, the banjo and the song,

Are courted yet by Afric's humble throng.
They drown their sorrows in a sea of mirth,
And crush young griefs as soon as they find birth
Neath dance's heel; and on the banjo string
A theme of hope, that forces woe to sing.
But one is there, to them a stranger born,
Whose manly brow the marks of thought adorn.
The low inventions of poor darkened mind,
Can never in the threads of nonsense bind
This mental Sampson; tho' by Slav'ry shorn
Of rightful manhood, weakness he doth scorn.
The abject sons of Afric's injured race,
With cabin sports assay to cheer his face,
But all in vain; their silly means repel,

Instead of please, the comrade they love well.
He's with them, but not of them; for the light
Of freedom flashing on him once, his sight
Has trained beyond low Slav'ry's bounds to ken
The hights, that he who treads will long to tread again.

All day he labors, speaking scarce a word;
All night lamenting in yon groves is heard.
His ear no more the torrent's voice shall woo,
In deep shades musing long, or wand'ring thro'.
His winding horn no more shall urge the chase,
Where the proud Wabash doth his woods embrace!
No more the flying stag shall dash the spray,
And bend the hawthorn from his mountain way;
And in the blossom'd fields of yellow sedge,
In thickets brown, or in the briery hedge,
His wary spaniel shall no longer spring,
Nor whirring grouse, nor partridge swift to wing!
His fields are gone! Farewell, ye sports of yore!
Ye goodly seats on Mississippi's shore!
And home is gone! All that makes labor sweet—
His hearth is darkened, where he once did meet
Bright chirping mirth around hoar comfort's feet.
No loving eye shall on his threshold wait,

No little footfalls meet him in the gate!
No faithful yard dog to the fence shall come,
To leap, and wag, and tongue his welcome home!
Dear Western home, a tender, last farewell!!

No more shall Rodney in thy bowers dwell.
Lo, in the cane and cotton, far away,
He bends to toil thro' all the sultry day!
Now on his life a weary journey takes
Thro' regions where no day beam ever breaks.
"Oh, God!" he mourns along the pensive hills,
"The rayless gloom that now my bosom fills.
My life ends here! existence tho', may creep
Some further on, but now ambitions sleep!"

Thus, all night once, alone he sighed,
In lanes and fields and forests wide,
And strolling on, was lost from view,
A deep dense pine shade wand'ring thro'.
There, where a bright stream leaping downward,
Moaned o'er falls and rambled onward,
Like a waywardness of childhood,
Or a wild dream; thro' the wildwood,
And within a farthest recess
Of the forest's leafy stillness,
Where the damp boughs stoop'd and listened,
And the waters flashed and glistened,
Formed a fountain clear, still, blue, deep,
In whose breast heaved Beauty asleep;
There, while morn was just awaking,
Slumbers from her eye-lids shaking,
And her mountain stillness breaking,
With her first sweet music making;

There, with eyes upon the ground bent,
Yet he onward mourning slow went.
All the waking woods were merry,
But his heavy heart was dreary.

So in deepening shades he wandered,
Where this wild strange stream meandered;
Knowing not, in his sad musing
Where he went, blindly not choosing
This or that path, as he went on
With his eyes the ground still bent on.
In his heavy soul he muttered—
These words pensively he uttered:
"Ah! bleak Norway's churl may feel not
To complain against his cold lot,
When he never knew a better;
And the naked son of Afric,
Led about from youth to manhood,
In his desert haunt and wildwood;
By the bloody hand of Traffic,
May not groan to wear a fetter;
But to him whose soul doth cherish
Longings that can never perish,
Who his arms in fetters galling
Feels, while liberty is calling
To her citadel before him,
With her bright skies bending o'er him;
But to him, how hard the fate is!

Ah, to him how dark the state is!
Earth her every pleasure looses
To his eyes, and hope refuses
All attempts to mount on high,
To her dwelling in the sky."
While thus he mourned in this sad plight,
Hard by his way, deep out of sight,
A sudden mighty stir he heard,
Of many a flapping bough and bird.
He upward glanced a hurried eye,
When thro' the parting branches nigh,
Upon the brooklet's other side,
A living beauty, lo he spied!
In native sweetness clothed, she stood
And all her fair proportions viewed

With fawn-like timidness. She deemed
Herself unseen, but watchful seemed.
Alone within her soft retreat,
The liquid mirror at her feet
Returned her beauty to her eyes,
Till, warmed with innocent surprise,
She stood admiring. Now her hand,
As graceful as a fairy's wand,
She waved above the prattling stream;
Then gentle as a reaper's dream,
She shook down raven locks of hair,
Upon the morning's dew-sweet air.

In deeper shades she now withdrew,
But Rodney's eyes as fast pursue.
There, half concealed, she looks more fair,
And seems abashed, at e'en the air,
That scarcely breathes upon her there.

*   *   *   *   *   *   *

A stolen glance at her fair parts,
Stripped Rodney's bosom to the darts
That Cupid's cunning strength let fly,
Till, wounded thro' his dazzled eye,
He sighed for breath, his bosom held,
To hush its leapings as it swelled.
He shut his eyes to look no more,
But looked, worse wounded than before.
Then thought to turn and steal away,
And thought, and thought, but yet did stay.
Her beauty like a full round moon,
Uncovered in the branches, soon
Appeared as fair as e'er was seen
That lovely orb, green hills between.
Then, step by step on tip-toe poise
She stole, and ev'ry little noise
To her had eyes. Back she withdrew
Within the shade, and now in view
Again in all her beauty rose,

And full and clear stood list'ning, close
Upon the marge, where grasses sweet

And blushing flow'rets kissed her feet.
The wanton waves that played below,
With am'rous descant ceased their flow,
And with a strangely pensive speech,
The maid to tarry did beseech.
A moment gazing on the flood
With Eve-like innocence she stood,
And watched her perfect image there;
While lost within her flowing hair
Her small hand rambled. She had now
Plunged in the panting stream below;
Had not the sudden thickets stirred.
The breathless maiden, shrinking heard
Some farmer's lad, on errand soon,
Towards her pipe his morning tune,
Quick as the lark, that, song-hushed darts,
When her still brush some footstep parts,
She, hasty dressed, deep out of sight
Within the thick boughs took her flight.
Rodney pursued, not knowing why,
Tho' oft to turn back he would try.
A power in his feet that drew
Resistless as the wind that blew,
Kept him a going, fast or slow,
And where, or how, he did not know.
Glance after glance his dazzled view,
Worse dazzled as the maiden flew

Beyond him, and as on he bent,
He knew not what his bosom meant,
In drinking breath on breath so fast,
And being out of breath at last.
But now his secret pleasure turned;
Ah! in the distance he discerned
His master skipping onward too,
To keep the coy sight on his view.

Then, Rodney turned and stole away,
And toiling, mourned the live long day;
But Mosher Aylor, stern as fate,
Pursued, till thro' the Brentfords' gate
He saw the beauty pass from sight,
Like some sweet vision of the night.

Now Aylor passed a wretched day,
And night's hours went their wingless way.
On all his house he closed his door,
And in a phrenzy paced the floor.
With hands behind him clasped, he stood,
Or leaning, sat, in sullen mood,
And sighed, and groaned, and raved with pain,
And rose and paced the floor again.
Till midnight's silence reigned around,
His discontent had reached no bound;
From his vexed sea he saw no shore,
He never had thus felt before.
His wonted bowl, for him had lost
Its deep oblivion, and crost
By broken dreams, his fevered breast,
Refused the arms of balmy Rest.
In this sad plight, a hideous cheer
Before him stood! The haggard seer
Of Aylor's shrine of wickedness,
Has heard the accents of distress,
That broke night's stillness, and has come,
To move the trouble burdensome.
Now Aylor spoke, when him he saw,
On whom he long had looked with awe;
"Here Micah! Micah! Micah! here!
To my complaint, oh lend an ear.
This morning as I strolled the wood,
Deep thro' yon cypress solitude;
Where shores of sweetest green ascend,
And thick boughs in the waters bend;
Fair as the light, I saw a maid
Unclothe her beauty in the shade.

I never felt a sting so bright;
I ne'er saw such an earthly sight.
Not radiant May with her perfumes,
And songs, and show'rs, and painted blooms,
And streams of crystal cheerfulness,
Could vie with her in loveliness.
But, like a bird of gorgeous hue,
She vanished on my starving view!"

"Aye," cries the seer, "no doubt have I,
That the same bird which you saw fly,
Is the fair Creole visiting
At neighbor Brentford's watering.
She is a slave, a waiting maid,
Brought down from New Orleans, 'tis said,"
"A slave! a waiting maid! a *queen*
Why don't you say; for ne'er was seen
A fairer cheek of Saxon hue
Nor prouder eye of brilliant blue.
Phoo, pshaw! a slave! a waiting maid!
That light-beam sweet from Heaven strayed?"
Loud cries the Seer, "A slave I know!
And can be bought as I shall show,
Dispel the phantoms of thy brain,
And turn to thy right mind again;
You must be sick!" "No," Aylor cries,
"I'm dead in love!" The seer replies,
Go pass in rest this far spent night,
And by the time young morn's in sight,
I'll bring the news to set thee right."

Now, Aylor, half consoled, adjourned
His thoughts till morn, and then returned
With Micah, to the Brentford seat,
The owners of the maid to meet.

The room was darkened where they met,
And all was quiet, save the fret
Of restless boughs, and whisp'ring leaves,

That mingle o'er the ancient eaves.
Now Aylor speaks, "For gold! for gold!
Aye, you but say she will be sold,
And you shall have your price all told."
Awed by the speaker's fiery eye,
The strangers whisper this reply:
"If her we sell, of this beware
She must receive your special care,
Not as a slave of low degree,
But as a ward, descended free.
And this day's doings, ever keep
From earth a secret hidden deep;
For should the news, by any means,
Escape your lips to New Orleans,
And reach our aged father's ears,
'Twill grieve away his few frail years..
Know this, he loves Leeona more
Than all his children ten times o'er.
His frailty has a passion grown,
And each day more his love has shown,
Till she has to us all become
The bane of pleasure, hope and home—
The idol of his feeble days,
The object ever of his praise.
Here to this wat'ring near your home,
He with reluctance let her come.

Now from *her* keep the fact concealed,
That she is sold: for if revealed,
She'll pine away, and droop and die,
Or from your house attempt to fly.
By wary speech, the truth we'll mask,
If our aged father ask;
"What hath befallen me? Where's my dear?
Why hast thou left my Ona there?"
This said, they drew aside and spake,
Concerning what price they should take;
And when agreed, they answered bold:
"Two thousand dollars down in gold!"

And Aylor with triumphant eyes,
Threw them their gold, and seized his prize.

With trembling hands they count their gains,
In haste divide with heartfelt pains;
For well they know a sister's tears,
And sweat, and blood, their purses fill.
Ah! well they know a sister's years,
Must now float onward at the will
Of him, who with a shameless (shamless) cheek,
To buy the hand of love would seek.
The offspring of a father's crimes,
The bitter fruit of broken vows,
The charming bloom of hapless climes,
The growth of unprotected boughs;
Within the grasp of blighting lust,

A lovely ruin now is thrust.
What tho' a father's heart shall break,
In spite of race Caste, taught to ache,
And yearn thro' age's kinder years,
For those to whom Nature endears;
What tho' he wakes with deepest groans,
What tho' his sleep with anguish moans?
When his first sorrow's bitter blast,
By soothing words is guided past,
His law-owned brood, will run at last
Their race in peace; tho' doomed by spite,
A sister thro' the stormy night
Of bondage mourn, a sad, sad sight.
What tho' his grief shall bow his head,
And while from view all pleasures sink;
He of a Quadroon's injured bed,
In age's twilight stand to think,
And often weep beside her grave?
Society will whisper "Slave!"

His love was wayward, and his wing,
Waved wand'ringly in life's warm Spring.

He saw the Quadroon, and they loved—
He and Leeona's mother, moved
Liked sounds of some wild instrument
Touched by the wind, and sweetly blent
Their lives in lasting pleasurement.
But Dame Caste turned her iron face,

And coldly frowned upon their course;
And drove sad love from faith's embrace,
With all the heartlessness of force.

'Twas thus by social interest's sullen voice,
Another's hands was made to be his choice.
And thus it is that many a love has grown,
Where even Christians dare make it known.
Where Hymen oft in gorgeous aspect shows,
From *true love* blossoms not a single rose;
While out in fenceless wastes of Nature spring,
Discovered only in wild wandering,
The purest blooms of love, whose fragrant breath,
Live thro' all life and linger after death.

A sister's life is signed away,
Her brethren can no longer stay
To see her drink the bitter cup,
Which they with sorrows have filled up.
Leeona kisses them good-bye,
Regards them with a tearful eye,
And long entreats them to make known,
Why she must there be left alone.
And then sweet as the fair-eyed dawn,
When her light steps first brush the lawn,
She meekly looked in Aylor's face;
And artless as a timid fawn,
With all of innocence's grace,

She reached a trustful hand in his,
A hand as pure as lilly is,
And gently followed, till from view
Within the Aylor seat they slow withdrew.

Now twilight waned and evening still,
Darkened the vales, while from each hill
Around came soft and lulling sounds.
From just beyond the vision's bounds,
One voice was heard sweetest of all,
And pensive as a late rain's fall
Through Autumn leaves sad and lone
The fading forests make their moan.
This was Leeona's, poor girl, torn
Away from childhood's hopes to mourn.
Aylor, meanwhile in sullen mood,
On his piazza list'ning, stood
Roving thro' mental solitude.
Full well he knew what Ona meant,
By her sad walks, and loud lament,
For he had caused it all.
His overtures of stark deceit,
She'd spurned and fled to this retreat,
To whisper in her Father's ear,
Complaints He ever stoops to hear.
So Aylor in Remorse's thrall,
Walked sullen thro' his ghostly hall,
Within a nook of vine shades went,

And o'er his thoughts in silence bent.
In Ona's heart though sad, there burned
A hatred deep, for all his aims;
And his entreaties, he discerned,
Were wind, and fanned the angry flames.
To her what were the Brazil's spicy breath,
Or India's sweet pride,
If life were fettered with a ghastly death,
That pained but never died?

This night too, Rodney wand'red forth to stroll,
And to the list'ning groves impart his soul.
The vision bright, that charmed his wayward dream,
Within this wood, beside the peaceful stream;
Returned when here he lingered. Now her home

To make at Aylor's she a slave had come,
And Rodney knew it not; for by caste barred,
He could not pass where wrong was standing guard.
But love hath ways that are past finding out,
And secret triumphs, that how brought about,
No one can tell. Love hath an open eye,
And watches little signs that others would pass by.

"I saw her here," thought Rodney to himself,
"'Twas here she flitted by coy as an elf,
And in yon boughs her disappearance made,
When wanton sounds disturbed the morning shade.
Could I but tell her. Ah! but fate forbids!
Poor Hope can't open there her dazzled lids.

Yet I *did see* her, oh, I saw her here!
And in my dreams she still doth bright appear.
Thank Heav'n there's none too crushed by wrong to see,
And beauty's the beholder's property."
But now his hope thro' darker clouds declines,
And thus within the sounding shade he pines:
"No more to me ere life's short race be run,
Shall e'er arise another happy sun.
How shall I break the vision that me wounds,
And drive it from my recollection's bounds!
A poor seafarer, and his star gone down,
From tempest-arms while clouds of heaven are thrown,
And wave-tossed danger wails to seize his bark;
Am I, now drifting thro' a wreck strewn dark.
Oh, why kind Heaven, plant within my breast,
A blooming sorrow—love begot unrest?
Content to bear tho' let me journey on,
Light yet may break life's dismal waste upon!
Now in the cypress gloom, he hushed his strain,
And homeward turned his mournful face again.

Eavesdropper winds, on errands from the South,
In sandals tripping, and with dewy mouth,
To Rodney turned, and whispered in his ear,

The broken murmurs of a sweet voice near.
A maiden sat within the fragrant shade,
And to the night this lamentation made:
"This life is all unreal as a dream,
 woes chase woes, like waves upon a stream.
Back yonder, just within the past I see
A bow'ry home, where hands do becon me,
To join the buoyant hearts of childhood's train,
And tread the blossom'd paths of hope again.
But here I am, away from home and friends,
While o'er my head a cliff of sorrow bends,
 Strange bodings haunt my pillow in the night,
And day uncovers terror to my sight.
But, whom I *saw* last eve within this shade,
Methought had by this time another advent made.
A strong companion of a troubled heart,
He seemed; oh, that to him I could impart
My woes; oh, that I could but see him once!"—here
She raised her eyes, and lo! the man was near.
Away she started at a frightened pace,
With red abashment kindling in her face.
Oh, was it real, could all this be true?
Was that the nymph, O what must Rodney do?
"Stay, maid!" he cries, "my wounded soul implores,
 Stay, fair one, stay! until my tongue explores
The hidden longings of a leaping heart;
Hear what a wounded spirit would impart."
Beyond the fence, and near the spring lawn gate,
Leeona paused, the speaker's steps to wait.
With timid mein, and from the other side,
Now Rodney leans, where blossomed vines divide,

And gathers words with anxious haste to tell,
The blushing beauty that he loves her well.
She answers with a sigh, and turns away,
And with her straggling locks begins to play,
Looks up again to speak, and only sighs,
But dazzles with the language of her eyes.
Then Rodney sighs, and leans, her hand to reach

A.A. WHITMAN

And press, that he may aid his falt'ring speech.
Her fingers touch him with a conquering thrill,
Her eyes could wound, her timid touch can kill.
He murmured something, *what*, no mortal knew,
And pressed the gate ajar, and stumbled thro';
And as Leeona sauntered slow away,
He whispered, but unheard, "Oh! angel, stay!"
"Oh, moon, speed on thy coming," then he said,
As blushing light beheld the tall slow maid,
Walk from the boughs, towards the mansion rise,
And flash around her over-pow'ring eyes.

Now Rodney's soul fair realms of pleasure knew,
And Time's face brightened as he onward flew.
All sights to him from sadness now awake,
For him the forests into music break,
Thoughts of Leeona speed the moments by,
And they with pleasure lighten as they fly.
His life was now a dream, in which care lay
Like labor's slumb'rous body, when the day
To night, and rest and lulling sounds gives way.
Thus many a day his burden down he threw,
And half the pangs of slav'ry never knew.
And thus it is, love hath a charm for life,
Whate'er the station, and whate'er the strife.
Where'er we roam, where'er our lot be cast,
In home's sweet shine, or in the raving blast,
Love to the soul a ray of light doth bring,
And scatter pleasures from his hopeful wing.
His advent lights up e'en the slave's poor shed,
And sweetens humble labor's daily bread.
Without thee, Love, what were the shepherd's reed?
Without thy blessings what the flow'ry mead?
From thy rapt fountain patriotism flows,
In thy fair province tall ambition grows,
Proud aspirations lean toward the skies,
And hight on hight great emulations rise.
Tho' fortune smile in some voluptous land,
Tho' fame weave laurels with a lavish hand,

The homely swain of Scotia's thatch-built shed,
Pines for his frugal meal of milk and bread,
Longs for his oaten tune and herded vales,
His shouting harvests and echoing flails.
And why? because sweet love can make him yearn
For early friendships, and his native bourne.

Some Sylvia charms the rustic's lowly dell,
The water sweetens from his native well,
The hills ennobles on his happy view,

His even plains with fresh delights doth strew;
The rough face brightens of his daily care,
With satisfaction crowns his scanty fare,
Pours pleasures in the lap of lusty toil,
And forces plenty from the stubborn soil.
To him, no hills above his own arise,
No vales so pleasant meet his ravished eyes,
And clouds so peaceful soften no serener skies.
To him no waters like the faithful rill,
That murmurs by his cot beneath the hill,
No tune so charming as his highland air,
No flocks so even, and no lambs so fair.
To him no land at all, no world besides
The world of love, that in his heart abides.
See where yon hero drives his way to war,
With Feast or Famine harnessed to his car.
O'er crumbled thrones, his flaming prowess lead,
And at his wheels imploring Commerce bleeds!
Some Cleopatra names the war-doomed lands,
And thrusts the torch of battle in his hand.

Night after night our lovers met and parted;
Night after night they grew more aching hearted,
Took moonlight rambles in the secret shade,
Wider and wider their excursions made,
And ev'ry night longer and longer stayed.
Oft arm-in-arm, with childlike dalliance, they,
And devious eyes, pursue their lonely way,

Or turn aside beneath the arching groves,
In scented nooks to prattle o'er their loves;
Till smiling thro' the drowsy branches bright
And peaceful, a late moon bids them "good night."

Again the shades of night were falling round,
And every hilltop now a speech had found,
When lost in bliss, the lovers met the moon,
Beyond their wonted rambles; but there soon
A crouching fury, who had scanned their walks
And drunk the whispers of their secret talks,
A master who can dare forbid their loves—
Flies on them like a hawk on thoughtless doves.
Leeona, clasping Rodney, starts and cries,
And Aylor hard to tear her from him tries;
Till Rodney's hand with warning aspect laid
Upon his shoulder, his hot rage allayed.
The shud'ring winds bore Aylor's threats around,
The groves their bosoms hushed to catch the sound,
But Rodney led his gentle Ona on,
And with her stood the threshold safe upon.

Now to her room, Leeona sauntered slowly,
A dim light on her table flick'ring lowly—
And sat awhile to ponder her sad heart;
A locket, gift from Rodney, took apart,
Looked on his picture, held it to her breast,
And with a sad, sad heart, assayed to rest.

Her light gone out, the room was dark, except
That thro' her lattice a shy moon beam crept
And looked into her troubled face, but fair,
That now upturned was still in fervent prayer.
She knew not that her faithful Rodney, near
The wall beneath, her lightest word could hear,
As thus she prayed: "Out of the storm, Oh, Lord!
Thou wilt bring shine to those who trust Thy word!
If draughts of bitter grief must first be ta'en,
Oh! Thou dost fill with brimming joys again!

Now in whatever land my Rodney mourn,
Or 'mid whatever trials he sojourn,
Like walls of strength around him, Oh, Thou King
Of Saints Thy mighty arms of succor fling!"
Lo! Rodney answers: "O, my Ona, dear,
If thou dost pray, I know the Lord will hear!"
Now to her feet the Creole bounds,
On tip-toe to the window steals,
Where blossomed vines her form conceals;
But clank of chains, and bay of hounds,
Stentorian oaths, and raving sounds,
Burst on her ear, and freeze her speech,
Ere yet her words can Rodney reach.

Now thronged about by twenty men,
And savage bloodhounds, nine or ten,
That howl with rage, and gnaw and bay,
Like demons that from Tophet stray,

Thro' nether worlds to wing their way.
Rodney, with irons loaded, she
Must turn away, or bear to see.
But as she turns, the hounds appear,
And in their deep jaws Rodney tear.
Unarmed he falls, with pain he groans,
gust of loud oaths mocks his moans,
While human monsters gather round,
And fierce dogs drag him o'er the ground,
Till he in cords of hemp is bound.
"Oh, save!" gasped Ona, as she, poor
Sweet child, sank swooning on the floor.
A moment there, a fair corpse seemed,
As in her face the sad moon beamed;
Then frantic rose, and down stairs flew,
And on her lover's bosom threw
Her wild sweet form, his stout neck drew
In her soft arms, and her cheeks fair
Nestled on his, and with her streaming hair,
Covered his bleeding shoulders that lay bare.

And this is Slav'ry! the wise faced creed,
That stretched a helping hand to Afric's need.
The holy Institution that was bound
To raise the heathen, tho' the Heavens frowned!
Ah! this was what a righteous Nation heard
Pray in her temples, and expound the Word.
This was Creation's good Samaritan,

And poor old Afric was the thief-torn man.
Oh, who has not the dear good shepherd seen,
Stand Moses-like, God and His hosts between,
Bless Slavery as a child from Heaven born,
Since Joseph was from poor old Jacob torn;
Watch ever sleepless, o'er his peaceful fold,
Unawed by dangers, uninduced by gold,
And weep if one poor lamb from shelter cries?
That is, one *white* lamb; if black, shut his eyes.
Ah! Young America, for God's sake, pause,
Hast thou such preachers, and hast thou such laws?

With ruffian hands, the maid was to her room
Forced hurriedly, and shut within its gloom.
Sad as the evening star's last glim'ring ray,
Now from a swoon, pale Ona crept and lay
Half conscious, till the night had far away
Towards the morning sped.
Wild phantoms wandered thro' her fevered brain,
Sweet slumber from her eyes its flight had ta'en,
And fainting hope had fled;
When in night's silent depths she heard a sound,
As of shy footfalls, that on tip-toe, wound
Along the mansion's stairs, now quick and low,
And now hesitatingly slow.
Then all was still, save that she heard
Upon the roof, light boughs that stirred,
And clasp'd at winds, that with them played,

And off in outer stillness strayed.
Again the cautious sounds revived,

And stood there motionless as death,
Till borne upon a husky breath,
This sentence thro' the key hole blew:
"Git up, my child, Ise cum fur you!"
'Twas "Aunt Ameriky,"—she knew—
She bounded up, she followed fast
Her sable guide, who hurried past
Her master's door with breathless ease,
And stood beneath the silent trees.

Then thus, low spake the good old guide,
"In yonder room is Rodney tied,
Where stands a locust on dis side.
De white folks sell him in de morn,
An he'll be left yer, shore's yer born,
Go see him gal, bid him farwell,
An' tell him what yers got to tell.
An' I'll stand here de outside by,
An' keep watchout wid open eye."
Now near this room—a prison made
In which to keep slaves till conveyed
Into their buyer's custody—
Leeona stole on cautiously.

Where thro' a crevice in the wall,
A late moon lighted up his thrall,

The pale maid saw her lover lie,
And called him with a burning sigh.
He answers: "Ah! is that my dove?"
And she, "Oh, have they bound you, love?"

The ebon angel of the night,
Now flew away and out of sight,
But soon returned with keys in hand,
And knife, and giving this command:
"Cum wid me, chile!" unlocked the room,
And entering its sepulchral gloom,
Stooped to her knees upon the floor,

The knotty fast'nings to explore
Of Rodney's arms; her knife apply,
And loosing him, let Ona fly
With outstretched arms to his embrace,
Lean on his breast and look into his face.

A moment passed, and drinking Ona's sighs,
The proud slave stood, while with his downward eyes
He caught the azure of her tender gaze,
And felt his kindling manhood all ablaze.
"Naught have I borne!" he cries, "love, but for thee,
These bloody tokens of the truth, oh, see!
Would I could Northward fly and now be free!
But where thou art not, all is bondage dire.
I'm free in chains, if I but in the fire
Of thy sweet eyes, may feel my heart inspire.

I now could arm, and would at once assay,
The vile destroyer of my joys to slay;
But then the law would drive me from thy sight,
Then day were darkness in my soul's long night."

Now thus Leeona, gazing in the moon,
"Haste, Rodney, lo, the day will open soon!
Hie to the cave, on yonder side extreme
Of that vast wood, where not the staunchest beam
Of potent noon can thy dark seat invade;
Keep hid by day, by night explore the shade.
There we shall meet. I'll there late rambles take,
And come to thee. The signal I will make
Is a low song, when there's no danger nigh,
Then we will walk; but hark, a footstep, fly!
Nay, come now dearest to this further shade,
Where our light converse may not be betrayed.
Tread lightly, ah! speak low, for now I fear
Suspicion walks abroad, with open ear
On night's still lips. Haste, Rodney, come away!
Still! there, thy heart unburden, make no delay.
List! hush! a hoof, 'tis—no—my beating heart;

That night bird, hark how lonely! Oh, I start!
For now methinks his note doth omens bring
Of sadness, all my poor heart saddening."
No evening shepherd ever tuned a lay,
Of sweeter accent, down his mountain way
Homeward returning at the close of day,

Than Rodney's speech was in Leeona's ears,
Till in the hall a certain step she hears.

His arms once more round 'Ona Rodney flings,
And sudden freedom to his flight lends wings,
Towards the cave he turns his flying face,
This way and that, and leaps at every pace,
To keep up with imagination's feet,
That brush by him in noiseless retreat.
The cave is reached, and wide apartments found,
With easy access, hollowed in the ground.
And ent'ring slow, now Rodney feels around,
Finds shelves of stone, and seats and beds of stone,
But windows, attics, and piazzas, none.

Meanwhile Leeona, noiseless as a sprite,
Flies thro' the halls, and up the ancient flight
Back to her room, and softly sinks to rest,
Till morn shall chase the darkness towards the West.
'Mid all the jars that shook the Aylor seat,
And hot suspicions, Rodney's dark retreat
Was ne'er discovered; and Leeona true
As only woman can be, 'scaping thro'
The darkness, met him oft, and took him food,
And gave him comfort in the dismal wood.
Of how she met him, cheered him; noble slave!
And lighted up the dungeon of his cave,
And with him walked thro' moonlight rambles long,

Cannot be painted in our faithful song.
Elijah, fed by ravens, it would seem,
Might have thought all the world a monstrous dream;

And Peter seeing wild beasts in a sheet
Tied up, and angel's crying "slay and eat,"
May have been awed at his supply of meat.
But what *must* he have thought, who chased by men
And hounds, from human sight into a den,
The angel of his love found stooping there,
Him to refresh, and his abode to share?

FLIGHT OF LEEONA

In bloom gemm'd depths, where Sylvan branches meet
Above dim paths, that thread a still retreat;
Where light on tip-toe shy, steals o'er your path,
Like some chaste maid unrobing at the bath;
There where old warrior pines on high doth tower,
In fashion quaint is built the Aylor bower.
Here 'Ona now a noon excursion made,
And wandered peaceful thro' the silent shade.
There, as she went, and could not turn nor stay,
But ling'ringly pursued her lonely way,
And gazed into the song-stirred woods beyond,
She stooped to raise a wayside flow'r with fond
And gentle touch, and with a sweet look try
To coax the timid azure from its eye.
And now she turns upon a mossy seat,
Where sings a fern-bound stream beneath her feet,
And breathes the orange on the swooning air;
Where in her queenly pride the rose blooms fair,
And sweet geranium waves her scented hair;
There, gazing in the bright face of the stream;
Her thoughts swim onward in a gentle dream.

Now, restless Aylor parts this dense retreat,
And 'Ona finds reclining, fast asleep;

While, save that one lone bird doth chirping peep,
Where's not a sound to raise its little feet
Within the stooping boughs—the very air
Seems half afraid to breathe upon her there!
And water lilies, prattling in the stream,
With speech subdued, enchanted list'ners seem.
Leeona's long locks round her slim waist meet,
The bright waves leap and sigh to kiss her feet,
While her reluctant breasts to view disclose
The lovely hues of life's serenest rose;

And timid rising, like twin moons do seem,
Just o'er the woody marge of some still stream.

Low Aylor peers the arching boughs beneath,
Lust heaves his bosom and compels his breath,
While thus he ponders, on his raving breast,
His hand in trembling indecision prest:
"I'll nearer steal, but then she might awake!
Oh, in these boughs I'll stand, till mine eyes take
Their feast of gaze! Ah! what a beauty she!
My soul is drowning in a boundless sea
Of what I can't express! And she is mine!
My own slave! No, Leeona, no, I'm thine!
I'll be thy slave, and thou my wife—my—no!
There's negro in her veins! 'Twould never do!
What Saxon hand a negro wench would woo,
And let disgrace frown on him? But she's fair!
Her cheeks, how radiant: ah! what eyes—what hair!

Thou angel slave! and mine! I'll nearer steal,
And make her while these boughs shall us conceal.
I'll proffer her a master's secret love,
Protection, freedom or her heart I'll move
To confidence and yielding secrecy,
By signs of stooped superiority."
Then, as some rough-armed hurricane that finds
The hiding places of the little winds,
Where insect horns their day long music keep,
And starts zephyrus in her noontide sleep;
So, filled with blasty lusts, now Aylor goes,
Till on the sleeper fair his footsteps close.
And as the fingers of a dream have caught
The waving pinions of her free young thought,
She hears his steps, sleep blends them with her dream,
Till touch'd, she wakes and bounds up with a scream.
Her master's low entreaties make her worse,
She screams for aid, till screaming makes her hoarse.
He grows more furious as she him defies;

The helpless lamb to flee the lion tries,
But fear o'ertakes her strength, and daunts her soul,
Her senses reel, and reason yields control
To blank unconsciousness, and what ensues,
Refrain to ask, Oh! man, withhold my muse!

The bower's deepest bosom saddened seemed,
As innocence's big libations streamed
Fast down Leeona's pity-suing cheeks,

And her poor breaking heart gave vent to shrieks;
And up to sympathizing Heaven she turned
Her tear-dimmed eyes, that with entreaty burned.
Oh, loveliness thou radiant visaged sprite,
Thou lute-voiced warbler wooing to delight!
By prince alike, and homely swain adored,
By every gentleness of soul implored!
When unprotected, howe'er cherished much;
To thee how blighting is the lewd hand's touch,
E'en as the woodside flow'ret plucked away—
Torn from the bosom of enliv'ning May—
Dost droop within the rough grasp of the swain,
Thou witherest to ne'er revive again!
And Slavery, thou worst of all the host
Of human ills, I loathe, and like thee most!
Thy name I spurn, thy grov'ling aims I hate,
And all thy bitter creeds abominate;
But like thee for the daughters thou hast borne,
The jewels that doth thy vile neck adorn,
The tender out-growth of unholy deeds,
The rich-hued blossoms of offensive weeds.

Here, reader, lies a lab'rynth on our way,
Thro' which perchance 'twould weary you to stray;
Or yet perhaps with some unwonted sight,
Or sound, mar all thy bosom's visions bright.
Our steps, therefore, around it now proceed,
Where to remoter realms our lovers lead.

But as we pass, there lingers on the ear,
A strong man's mournings for his lover dear.
For Rodney hears that his fair 'Ona's dead,
And sleepless anguish bows his manly head,
The nightly forests hear his wand'ring cries,
And with her stony speech his cave replies.

'Twas eve in Florida serene and bright,
And gently sighed the wind as sighs a maid
When watching in an early moon's round light,
Her lover's footsteps in the trysting shade.
The woods breathed softly, and their even breath
Was sweet with blossoms of the neighb'ring heath.
And, save the lonely note of nightingale,
The churlish out-bursts of the farm boy's vale,
The horn owl's shout, and swamp bird's lone reply,
No evening sound disturbed the sleepy sky.

Now near a dark and solemn wood,
Close by the Aylor house I stood.
The evening star, without a peer,
Was sinking in his mild career,
As sinks the warrior on his shield,
When vict'ry holds a silent field,
And no alarum breaks his rest,
To build her watch fires in his breast.
Soon, as a maid will half conceal
To show her beauty, then with sighs,

Languishing looks, and yielding eyes,
Will arm her sex with that appeal,
Which conquers him who dares to feel;
So, bursting from the wood's embrace,
A moon in soft clouds dipped her face,
Ascended then her peaceful throne
Of green hills, and supremely shone.

I heard a wail of woman's woe;
Now loud it bursted, and now low,
Suppressed, as if in sudden flow,

A hand had checked its bitter gush;
Then followed an expressive hush,
When, in the mansion's silent hall
I saw a female proud and tall,
Half covered in the myrtle's shade,
Thro' which the moonlight faintly strayed.
Her long hair stream'd below her waist
In wild waves; and her bosom chaste
Arose in pensive sweetness, bare,
Beneath a face that pale with care,
Some monster trouble seemed to dare.
Her eyes with sullen lustre blazed,
As up in Heav'n's still face she gazed,
And clasped an infant to her breast,
To gently hush its sweet unrest.
I nearer to the woman stole,
And lo! she was the fair Creole!

For unobserved, I reached the hall,
And leaned against the shadowed wall,
Just as the moon was fairly seen,
Breaking white banks of clouds from 'tween.

I heard the Creole's softest sighs,
And saw her flash her restless eyes
Upon her rear; I now did know
There was concealed some dreadful foe.
I looked upon her lovely form,
And felt my hurried blood run warm.
Ah! she was beautiful, tho' not
So fair as lovesick rhymers plot,
Or whining prose mongers array,
Among the novel's little way,
Through which good sense doth never pass,
But where the intellectual ass
Delights to roam, or fast or slow,
To see the strange *white lilies* grow,
Or hear a big black giant blow!
Ah! not *so* fair, but a rich rose,

And brilliant as the stream that flows
From Summer hills, with meadows sweet,
And dewy corn-fields at their feet;
While bleating pastures peaceful lie,
Beneath an azure canopy.

But hovered o'er by raven-winged fears,

Assailing wrongs had dried her tears
In their bright home; tho', as the rill,
When Winter from his cheerless hill,
Freezes the surface with his breath,
But cannot stop the flow beneath;
So her proud look of beauty showed
That sorrow's stream beneath it flowed.

Oh! how I wished I knew wherefore
Her wrongs, and her distresses sore!
How then I could have met her foe,
And brought her weal, or shared her woe!
I raised my hands, I strove to speak,
But long suspense had made me weak;
I could but lisp a single word,
And *that* too faintly to be heard.
Then, ere I caught my reeling sense,
I would have sprung to her defense,
But horror froze my sluggish blood,
And I aghast in silence stood.
A whisper low breathed thro' the hall,
And then there came a quick footfall.
Leeona flashed a hurried eye,
And "Oh, my Rodney!" then did cry,
And to his brave arms weeping fly.
A moment clasped in love they stood;
Then he looked round in sullen mood,
As calm as night, but stern as death,

Resentment warming every breath,
And "fly, Leeona!" quickly gasped,
And to his lips her small hand clasp'd.

"They're on us now, and soon we'll be
  Beyond the reach of Liberty."

"Hush! there they come! can't you hear
  Their angry footsteps hurrying near?
  Wait not a moment to be gone,
  By Heaven aided fly alone!
  I'll meet, and hold them here at bay,
  Or stain with blood their fiendish way."
  I strove now but could not withdraw,
  Nor look, nor shut my eyes for awe.
  A hurried sigh, a sob suppressed,
  Escaped Leeona's noble breast.
  All earth to her was in her arms,
  And she could tread on Scorpion harms,
  While this firm purpose swelled her heart—
  To *live not* from her babe apart.
  Now wild as the wild cat'ract moans,
  Thro' deep shades and replying stones,
  The murmur from her bosom rose:
  "God save my Etta from her foes!"
  Then on her shoulder swinging straight,
  The thoughtless infant's little weight,
  Forth from the mansion' s hall she stole,
  Like hope's last vision from the soul.

  Her lips were clenched, her dark eyes staid,
  Her brow was knit and arched with shade,
  To Heaven's arms she looked for help,
  And fearless as the lion's whelp,
  Was winding thro' the silent grove,
  With no cheer but the moon above.
  Now fast and faster onward flew,
  Till indistinct upon the view,
  She seemed a shadow, then was seen
  No more the darkling trees between.

  Now in the dismal mansion roared
  A storm of heavy steps that poured

From aisle to aisle, and hall to hall,
As if loud tongues in every wall
Were loosed upon the night to call.
The current foamed towards the door,
From which had fled the Creole poor,
And o'er the voices of the crowd
One great grum throat was heard aloud,
Like a crack'd trumpet madly blown,
Or like a fierce boar's sally groan.
"Let loose the hounds upon her track,
Go, villains (villians)! Speed and bring her back!
Or leave her torn upon your way,
And on her flesh let vultures prey!"

Now Aylor ceased, and his dread form,

Peerless in terror, issued forth,
As wrathful as the dark browed storm
That shuts the doorway of the North,
And drapes the eagle's palace bright,
In curtains of the misty night,
Then grum as some old Indian king,
He strode among the gaping throng
Till like a Champion of the ring
Of loud Olympus, stern and strong,
Of matchless port, and manner proud,
He rose above the gaping crowd
Of men and dogs, and shook his hair.
Dread silence seized the trembling air,
Dumb terror made his minions quake,
Their knees to smite, their fingers shake,
And dogs beneath his nod and scowl,
Began to gnaw their chains and howl.

The chains are loosed, and at a smack,
Away fierce yelping fly the pack.
Their deep, loud throats in full chase break,
The darkling woods responsive speak,
And far off hills from slumbers wake.

The very night shades seem to fly,
And dance and flutter on the eye;
For dreadful sight is it to see,
A woman from swift bloodhounds flee.

Then like some lion, when loud dogs invade,
That flies ferocious from his roaring shade,
His bristling kindred scatters from his path,
And shakes the forests in his lordly wrath;
So now brave Rodney from his cover springs,
And right and left her loud pursuers flings.
These at him stare with trembling fears opprest,
He plucks a dagger from his heaving breast,
Displays the ghastly warning to their eyes,
And in pursuit of hounds and Creole flies.

Ah! ye whose eyes with pity doth run o'er,
When mournful tales come from a heathen shore,
Of babes by mothers thrown to crocodile;
The scaly terror of the languid Nile;
Of Brahma's car and Islam's wanton rites,
And bloody raids on Zion's sacred hights!
Ye who hear these and pray for God to come,
Behold yon mother fleeing from her home!
A master's child upon her frantic breast,
And by a master's savage bloodhounds prest;
And this, too, where in every steepled town,
The crucifix on human wrong looks down!
Think then no more of heathen lands to rave,
While in America there breathes a slave!

Rodney pursues, and where the sickened moon
Looks thro' the woods, comes on the Creole soon.

The angry hounds have overta'en their prey,
And round Leeona, madly mingling, bay.
Deep thro' the wastes their fiendish voices ring,
Fierce with their tongues, wood, plain and hillock sing;
And now they close upon her, thick around;

Ah! God, they seize and drag her to the ground!
Lo! Rodney nears, he hears his 'Ona's cries,
Right on the hounds with flashing steel he flies;
They on him furious turn, with eyes that glare
Like furies' fell, jaws gaping, and teeth bare;
This one and that he seizes as they lunge
Upon him, and their dread fangs in him plunge.
Deep thro' their reeking sides his blade he drives,
They reel away and empty out their lives;
Till with their warm blood dropping from his hands,
He master of the situation stands!

Ah! ye whose hearts with swifter currents beat,
When fabled gods in equal combat meet,
Shout loud the challenge, swing their shields immense,
While armies hang around in dread suspense,
Lift their vast lances, like the lightnings driven,
Jar all the plain and shake the vault of heaven;
Behold this hero of the real fight,
This *man* who dares the wiles of swampy night;
Whose fearless bosom, lit with valor's fire,
Withstands the monster bloodhound in his ire;
Whose faithful heart to love's first impulse true

Will dare to suffer and is brave to do.

Now Rodney listens, his surrounding views,
And thro' the pines his dismal way pursues.
Leeona follows on his journey dark,
Where night-owls laugh and wary foxes bark;
Till thro' the branches op'ning day's in sight,
With rosy smiles and locks of streaming light.

We wander now in grasses long and damp,
O'er oozy mosses of a dismal swamp,
Thro' languid brakes, and under monster trees,
Thro' whose vine loaded boughs *noon* never sees.
Here nature sleeps her long, long torpid nap
In silence, on the Tropic's tangled lap;

Here yellow streams with lazy murmurs creep
On slowly, talking in their sluggish sleep;
Here hideous reptiles in their slimy reign
Crawl aimless ever, and an apish train
Of forest hoodlums day long orgies hold;
And birds, although their plumage gleam with gold,
And divers colors, sing not; in this wood,
This habitation of dark solitude,
Our lovers, for their lives escaping, fly
Into the arms of dismal safety.
The scaly venom of the pathless brakes
About them here a sure protection makes,
For who will dare the danger of the bogs?

And here is crocodile a match for dogs.

Here hope our lovers found,
And love about them wound
Her silver cords the tighter;
As fears vanish'd away,
And they from day to day
Felt life's burdens grow lighter.
Ona saw Rodney's manhood, he
Her fortitude and constancy;
Thus, each could in the other see
Enough to keep the loving eye
With pleasures running over.
As Eve and Adam, innocent
Within the charms of Eden went,
And nothing of the wide world knew,
Save what lay just betwixt the two;
So wandered these, the wild shade thro',
Lover absorbed in lover.

Far from their home within the wood,
Once Rodney went to search for food,
And ready make, for he next day
Must toward the North Star take his way.
Leeona biding, sandals knit

Of fibres from the cypress split,
A basket rude of willows wove,
And gathered fruits within the grove.

Thus wand'ring round, she missed her track,
And lost, could not her way find back.
At last despairing, sad she stood,
Then on her devious way pursued,

The sun upon his western way,
Had nearly reached the verge of day,
Baptizing in his orange sheen
The lofty groves of cypress green;
When in the swamp grass, long and dank,
Leeona reached some bayou's bank.
Lo! all around was strange and lone,
And silence on her dismal throne
Held her dark sway in every nook;
Save that one swamp bird yonder, shook
A mournful noise from his throat,
That sounded something like a note;
And that one tiny wren did say
Some feeble things anear her way,
Scarce able when it flew to shake a spray.

Leeona turned to scan the wood,
When lo! beyond her scarce a rood,
A horrid human form she viewed!
A tall old man in skins half guized,
Half savage and half civilized,
With a great cudgel in his hand,
Towards her gazing still did stand.

About his waist a leathern thong
Bound his long locks, they were so long.
Uncombed and matted close they lay,
And age's touch had made them gray.
His gaunt arms were of monstrous length,
The ghastly signs of wasted strength.

"Ah!" Ona sighed, "What shall I do?"
And, as she thought, unseen, withdrew;
But slow the ghostly hermit stalked
Around her hiding-place, then walked
Straight in the bush to where she lay
Breathless, stood squarely in the way,
Swung his great cudgel round and round,
Chattered and gnashed, and stamped the ground,
Rolled his wild eyes, growled like a bear,
And thrust his fingers in his hair.

A true heroine of the cypress gloom,
Now there to lie, the Creole saw her doom—
A reckless madman had her in his hand—
She sprang up, and did at his elbow stand,
And cried out, "Look sir, see my pretty child!"
At this, the raving specter grimly smiled,
Let fall his cudgel, muttered some strange speech,
And for the babe his dreadful claws did reach.
"Have you seen Nanawauea?" then he cried,
"She died long time ago, and then I died;
Who wrongs the red man, wrongs the race of man;

You hurt my wigwam now, sir, if you can!"
Leeona answered, pointing him away,
For no auspicious moment long will stay:
"Your Nanawawa lives in yonder glen,
Make haste and find her—come and tell me then."
Now both hands in his hair the madman threw,
Dashed off and laughed, and gibbered as he flew.
"Dark mystery," Leeona leaving, said,
"Hath in that human waste her mansion made!
Ah! now within his once love-lighted breast,
The owly phantom builds her broody nest.
And that high seat where wisdom once did dwell,
Is now inhabited by visions fell,
And recollections harrassing, among
Which, a dreadful secret holds her tongue!
And 'Nanawawa;' love-balmed name survives—

Above that heap of mental ruins lies!
Poor wretch, unconscious of existence save
With the loved dead, thinks he's beyond the grave!
'Who wrongs the red man.' Why he speaks of wrongs,
To that the secret of his words belongs;
Wrong! wrong! Yea wrong! We all that monster know,
The blight and bane of earth, and source of woe!

Now Rodney's voice and heavy footsteps broke
Upon the Creole's ear, as thus he spoke:
"Leeona, here am I! What were those sounds?
And what went by me with such dreadful bounds?"

Leeona told him; list'ning still he stood,
Then talking low they slowly left the wood,
Began their steps toward a Northern clime,
And looked on Florida for their last time.

THE RUNAWAY

Awake, my muse, ye goodly sights among,
The land of Boone and Kenton claims my song.
Thro' other scenes our lovers take their flight,
See where their wand'ring footsteps pass in sight.
Lo! where yon pleasant valleys meet the eyes,
And goodly hills their forests lifting rise!
Here, as we pass, along our cheerful way,
Small farms adjoining, stretch in green array.
And small farm houses, looking great trees thro,'
And neat dressed orchards, dot th' enlivened view;
And their quaint roofs by Autumn suns embrowned,
With wind-mills rude, and bird-box turrets crowned,
Look thro' the branchy elms and locusts high,
And send a rustic welcome to the eye.

See where yon flocks their even pastures browse,
And lowing homeward, hear the sober cows,
And hear yon plowman whistling as he plows.
Here circling plenty meets returning suns,
And lucid cheer in ev'ry valley runs,
Loud satisfaction fills the evening air,
And jovial comfort soothes the ear of care.

Thrice hail! proud land, whose genius boasts a Clay!
The Cicero of slavery's palmy day,
The gifted champion of Compromise,
Whose mien majestic filled a nation's eyes;
And on the eloquence of whose wise tongue
A learned Senate in rapt silence hung;
A Senate, too, whose fame no one impugns,
Of Websters, Randolphs, Marshals and Calhouns.
And could a land that boasts a mind like this—
That bord'ring on the clime of freedom is—
Suffer a harlot with her whorings vile
To peacefully pollute her gen'rous soil?

Yes, green Kentucky with her native pride,
Proclaiming trust in the great Crucified,
Flaunting her prestige in the world's wide face,
Boasting descent and precedence of race,
And by the greatest of all statesmen led,
Shared the pollutions of a slavish bed.
All o'er her fields, the blood-hound's savage bay
Pressed the poor sable trembling runaway,

And sometimes by the home of Henry Clay!
In all her woods, the wail of wild distress
Was heard, as tattered starving wretchedness
Fled in the shrieking wrath of wintry storm;
Wrapping her babe in rags to keep it warm!
Can I forget the tears a parent shed
When her dear hand she placed upon my head,
And me embracing, tremulously said:
"My heart is sick whene'er the sad winds blow,
And all the ground is buried deep in snow,
For I remember, when I was a child,
The night was dark, the raving winds were wild,
The earth was still, the snow lay deep and white,
When at our door there came a footstep light.
We opened, and a strange black woman's face.
Looked in; she held a child in her embrace
And said: "Ize nearly froz to deaf', oh wont
You let me in? Oh! don't say *no!* Oh don't!"
She came in, but before we said a word,
Her master's voice was in the quarters heard!
She knew the sound, her babe close to her drew,
And back into the wintry tempest flew.
The morning came, and chilly miles away,
In snow half hid the lifeless mother lay!
But in her arms the babe alive did sleep,
And when discovered, woke, but did not weep!
And lo! uncovered to the mournful light,

'The mother's face was black—the babe's was white!"

I love Kentucky; tho' she merit scorn
I can't despise the land where I was born.
Her name I cherish, and expect to see
The day when all her sons will cherish me.
Her many sins have all in common been
With other sisters' who their sins have seen.
Yes, I will pray for that good time to come
When I can say: Kentucky is my *home*.
And this I now ask at my country's hand,
If I must die in some far distant land,
Then let my countrymen, when I am dead,
Where I was born, make my eternal bed.

But here our lovers are again;
Awake, my muse, thy wonted strain!
The hounds at day-break struck a trail
In deep Green River's lonely vale,
And thro' the dusk of dewy morn,
Echoed the hunter's rousing horn.
"What is it?" flew from tongue to tongue,
As to his horse each rider sprung.
A moment in their saddles still,
They heard the baying on the hill
Not far away, and full well knew
A runaway before them flew,
The chase began, the horses dashed

Away, and thro' the bushes crashed,
Like birds that flutter on the wing
All thro' the wild copse scattering.
Each horseman pressing for the lead
Bore on and on, with champing speed.
On, on and on, and on, o'er hills,
And winding valleys, leaping rills
And fallen trunks like startled hinds,
Wild as a flood, as swift as winds.
The hounds' loud clamor rolled and broke
Morn's drowsy stillness, and awoke
The sleepy hills, that answered back

The lusty tonguing of the pack.
Within his quiet farmhouse wood,
The early rustic list'ning stood,
The plowman whistling in his lane,
Paused, listened, paused and paused again,
Surmised, went on, went on, surmised,
And at their loud speed stood surprised;
As o'er his fences passing near,
He heard them in their mad career.

Their loud tongues on the morning breeze
Now Rodney heard, as if the trees
Were yearning in their sympathy,
And stretched, and sighed and whispered "fly."

And fly he did, and as away he sped,

Soon of the pack a length'ning space ahead;
His nimble limbs grown strong by punishment,
Bore manly up as on and on he went.
O'er fences high, and gullies wide he leapt,
Skimmed level fields and thro' the briars crept,
Now pricked by these, now by the wanton thorn,
And now by knotty bamboos hung and torn.
His footsteps now had gained a wooded hight,
Now fields and houses all were out of sight;
He paused to listen, heard his heart's quick beat,
And thought. it was the sound of coming feet.
Another instant and the flying slave,
Was trying if his legs could well behave.
Thro' pond'rous woods and darkling shades he ran,
Three miles or more from where his flight began,
Sometimes along the wild boar's narrow way,
Sometimes where hunted wolves in cover lay.
He soon could hear the fierce hound on his rear,
Baying out inbred hate, and drawing near.
Loud in the distance angry signals wound,
And furious yells urged on the flying hound.

Dread oaths were muttering on the morn's still air,
Enough to hush the jungle's roaring lair.

Now Rodney, bursting from the wood,
An instant on the high bluffs stood
And gazed upon Green River's flood,
That tossed and growled and rolled beneath,

Like torments in the vaults of death.
The rocks look'd down with angry awe,
And feeble shrubs leant back and saw.
Few moments more the worst must bring,
For now the worst had poised its wing!
The hounds are on him! "Save! oh save!"
Right downward leaping cries the slave,
But not into a watery grave!
With arms of steel he mounts the wave,
He grapples with the dizzy tide,
Turns downward, where the cliffs doth hide,
And then with strokes manful to see,
He pulls for life and liberty.
Meanwhile the hounds have ceased to bay,
The hunters look and turn away,
And "Ah! *he's* drowned!" all seem to say.

Three nights or more curtain the skies,
And now we turn our weary eyes
To where the Creole mother flies.
Thro' dangers led by friends at night,
By day concealed from mortal sight,
Thus far, secure has been her flight.

A storm was low'ring, and the sun was low,
The Creole's weary steps were short and slow,
The air grew sightless, and the fields were still,
The woods were restless on the solemn hill,

The earth seems shrinking from the threat'ning skies,
As night on rayless wings athwart the sun's path flies.

All nature trembles! Lo! the cloud-folds break,
The mountains with their thunder-tongues awake,
While livid lightnings glare on every peak,
And with their arms of flame, their warring lances take.
The startled clouds flee out into the deep
Of troubled night; and headlong down each steep
Rush dizzy torrents from the flood-drenched hills,
And foam along the overflowing rills.
But hark! in all this storm a woman's wail!
A mother's anguish doth the ear assail!
Beneath yon beetling rocks, oh raise thine eyes,
To where Leeona lifts her tender cries!
See now she sinks into the cliff's embrace,
And turns to heaven her entreating face
In tearful beauty! Hark! for help she cries!
And thunders answer from the wrathful skies!
Between the surges of tumultous winds,
Her cry a passage thro' the tempest finds.
"Oh God! my child! my child!" she wails distrest,
And clasps the tender sorrow to her breast.
But like the vaulty whispers of the tomb,
Her words come back from hollow-throated night's deep gloom.
Oh! Heaven, can'st thou thus be pitiless,
And hear, unmoved, the cry of loveliness?

Cause thy rebellious winds to war no more,
The loud disturbers of a nightly shore!
Ah! how the torrents now are pouring down,
They seem as if the whole earth they would drown;
But this last flood descending, hope creates,
For when it slackens, then the storm abates.

The rain has ceased; but the belabored wood
Yet waves and trembles in a troubled mood.
The frantic Creole lifts a piercing cry,
Hoping to rouse some woodsman dwelling nigh;
But in the bluffs above her wolves reply.
"Oh! Heaven," shrinking in the rock she gasps,
And in her arms her infant tighter clasps,

"The wolves are howling, Ah! What shall I do?
Beset by beasts and human monsters too!"
Then like some doe when dogs and horns surround,
That starts, stops, listens, starts with sudden bound,
Flies from her covert, leaps rock, fence and hedge,
And leaves the baying dangers of the sedge.
Right so Leeona stops, and starts, and leaps,
And bounding onward leaves the howling steeps.
The flashing heavens make her footing good
In darksome paths, through the abodeless wood,
As on she flies, a spirit of the night,
But knows not where her heaven assisted flight.

Day came—an ugly, wet and sluggish day—

When in the woods, far on Leeona's way,
A band of sun-browned cleavers she beheld,
That near their lonely homes their forests felled.
Their great rough arms, as rough as oak limbs are,
Dropt on their knees, and to their elbows bare;
Held up their chins, as from their logs they gazed
Upon the fleeing woman, sore amazed.
And when she came to them with tales of woe,
They pressed around her eagerly to know
From whence she was, and whither she would go.
And then they grouped and muttered to themselves,
Smote on their breasts, and seized their pond'rous helves,
And breathing out a gale of oaths and threats,
They led her to their humble forest seats.

Of how the Creole, by these woodsmen's (woodsmens') aid,
Her further flight toward Ohio made;
Of how she wandered two long months, beset
By shrewd suspicions, and by mistrust met,
By day concealed, by night hurried along,
Cannot be uttered on the tongue of song,
But raise your eyes to where the verging land
Of Bondage touches Freedom's holier strand.

Low in the cheerless West, deceitful rays
Kindle their fires to a feeble blaze.
The leafless woods send up a ceaseless howl,
As looking down upon them with a scowl,

From voiceless hills, the wintry blasts doth stand,
And shake their shrieking tops from hand to hand.
The hoarse Ohio chafes his bleak shores gray,
And sullen, rolls to warmer climes away.

But list! is that the moaning of a gale
Disconsolate, within yon leafless vale?
Draw nearer, listen, now it rises high,
Now lower sinks, recedes, and now comes nigh.
Is it the blast of all its mildness shorn?
Ah! no, 'tis poor Leeona that dost mourn!
See where on yonder rising rock she stands,
And holds her tattered garments in her hands;
Scarce able to rescue them from the wind,
That flings them, with her streaming locks behind;
Unwraps her perfect limbs, that white and bare,
Empurple in the bitter Northern air.
From her bare feet blood trickles down the stone!
Ah, God! Why is she here? Why thus alone?
Oh, what hath driven her from home away,
And Comfort's hearth, upon this ruthless day?

Ah! see her driven from warm Care's embrace
A lone sweet exile of the Creole race!
By heaven forsaken, and denied by earth,
As if too crime-stained to deserve a birth.
By native streams no more in peace to rove,
And hear the sylvan music of the grove.

No more to pluck the fruits of gen'rous growth,
And gather flowers of the fragrant South,
How can she meet the fierce wrath of the North,
Houseless and clotheless, thus to wander forth?
Ah! Ask you? Turn to where yon hounds pursue,

And circle swift the clam'ring forests thro.'
Hark! how loud horns resound upon her rear,
Oh! heaven save her! Is no helper near?
Must she beneath the angry tide be borne,
Or by the savage hounds be seized and torn?

Beyond the river is a fisher's hut,
Close in a cove beneath tall forests shut;
Beyond the hut a narrow path climbs o'er
The crescent bluffs, and winds along the shore.
Within this hut Ben Guildern sate all day,
Mending his nets and lines, and smoked away.
He dreamed of this wide world and all its cares,
Its hopes and doubts, its pleasures, pains and snares,
Of man's pilgrimage to a better bourne,
Where toil shall rest, and man shall cease to mourn;
And of the days and other faces gone,
Ere he was left to pass thro' life alone;
Of pleasant tasks his manly arms had wrought,
Of slumbers sweet that toil remitting brought;
And of the many times he climbed that hill,
And found a wife and children waiting still;
And supper smoking, and a ready plate,

When all day's luckless toil had made him late.
"All gone!" within his wave-tossed soul he sighs,
And o'er the waters lifts his tear-dimmed eyes,
"A cold and blustry night the boat went down,
And my poor wife and babes were left to drown!"

He sees a signal from the other shore—
A woman beckons him to set her o'er;
He hears the hounds, and not a word is said,
A fugitive he sees imploring aid;
His boat is launched, and from her moorings thrown,
The tide awaits her, rolling up and down,
A moment near the shore she slow doth move,
And waits another and another shove;
This way and that the eddy smooth she tries,

Ventures and darts, and with the current flies.
So when the speedy roe is brought to bay,
Where rising cliffs oppose her woody way,
Within some nook embraced by rocks and logs,
She turns her head upon the bristling dogs,
Bends here and there until her way is clear,
Flies through her foes and leaves them on the rear.

Seized by the heaving tide, the feath'ry boat,
Midway the river down begins to float,
But Guildern with his strong arms grasps the oars,
Plies all his strength, and up the current soars.
The angry billows clamor at his keel,

And on his prow in sudden fury wheel,
Till, at an angle of a good degree
Above the hound-pressed Creole pausing, he
Wheels short his flight, athwart the current shaves,
And shoreward glides before the rolling waves.
So when the untiring mistress of the winds
Discovers in the covert feeding hinds,
Midway she meets the current of the skies,
And by its adverse strength succeeds to rise,
Till high above the destined point she swings,
Drops from the clouds and shaves on level wings.

The shore is touched, the Creole boards the boat
With child in arms, and all are now afloat.
Old Guildern speaks not, but plies all his skill,
And looks the firm monition, "now be still,"
Leeona's heart with hope and awe is swelled,
She meets an eye that danger never quelled,
A face as rough as wintry hills, but bland,
An arm of massive strength, but gentle hand,
And mien of dreadful soberness, that braves
The sullen fury of the wind and waves.
The boat is now far out into the stream,
And as her quick oars in the low sun gleam,
Rides up and down the wave, and o'er and o'er,

And level swims towards the other shore.
Ah! nobly bearing up her precious freight,
How steadily she rocks beneath the weight!

Her keel has touched, it cleaves the yellow sand,
Thank God! thank God! they land, they land! they land!

Within a fisher's hut all night,
And leaving by the early light
Of bleak December's lurid morn,
Leeona passes into sight,
Cast down and faint, and travel-worn.

From naked hills loud shrieking flew the blast,
And out of hearing moaned along the waste,
Like some torn beggar all disconsolate,
That mutters from harsh Opulence's gate;
As 'Ona trudged along her lonly way,
Beneath a nightly vault of starless gray.

Her murmuring infant shivered in the blast,
As houses by her way she hurried past,
Where rustic comfort sat with smiling pride,
At honest labor's genial fireside.
Thus thro' the hoary landscape's wintry scorn,
She forced her mind's consent to journey on till morn.

The clouds dispersed as night wore slowly on,
And stars from their high glist'ring fields looked down,
Till late the moon-top'd hills in white arose,
And peerless night unveiled her shivering realms of snows.

Ah! bent and trembling, see that gentle form,

Where shelt'ring rocks oppose the wrathful storm,
Chased like some beast, that hovers with her young
In yawning caves, and desert rocks among.
Her tender infant in her arms is prest,
Hushed are its cries—it gently seems to rest.

Where vagrant swine their wintry beds have made
Of leaves and branches from the forest shade,
Now 'Ona stoops to rest her darling's head,
When lo! she starts, she shrieks—her child is dead!
Her wounded bosom feels a nameless dart,
A ghastly sorrow clutches at her heart—
Nor fear assails, tho' now to leave she tries,
But trying stays, her babe embraces, cries,
The cold cliffs groan, and hollow night replies.
The dismal gorges murmur at the sound,
And empty fields spread echoless around.

Beside her babe the weeping mother kneels,
With anguish dumb its pulseless hands she feels;
Its placid cheek against her face is prest,
Her ear is leant upon its silent breast;
Her hopes are gone! and Heaven's pure ear hears
Deep grief entreating thro' a flood of tears.
Above the cliffs where winds a country way,
A voice is heard in cautious tones to say:
"Leeona! Oh Leeona! Oh my dear!
Is it my 'Ona's mournful voice I hear?"

The Creole hushed, afraid to trust her soul,
That felt a mighty burden sudden roll;
Quick claspt her bosom in aching suspense,
But now distincter heard the voice commence:
"Leeona! Oh, my 'Ona! are you near?"
The Creole answers, "Rodney, I am here!"
Rodney had heard along Leeona's way,
Of her wild flight, and her pursued all day.
Now down the cliffs in breathless haste he flies,
And clasps his life, as thus to him she cries:
"Oh! see, my Rodney; see where baby lies!"

The bosom that had life-long sorrow borne,
The heart which had so long been taught to mourn,
With *real* manly sympathetic heaves,
Bent o'er the little corpse and raised it from the leaves.

"Poor harmless comer!" then he gently said,
"Better for thee that thy pure soul has fled
With angel watches to the waiting skies,
Where peace e'er flows, and happier climes arise.
Conceived in trouble and in sorrow born,
Thy life rose clouded in its very morn,
And wore along with unpropitious suns;
But to a happy close at last it runs!
Sweet be thy rest upon this lonely shore,
Rocked in the cradle of the winds no more,
And ne'er awakened by the tempest's roar."

This said, to roll the stone away he stoops,
And in its bed a hasty resting scoops,
Commits his tender burden to the ground,
In poor Leeona's last torn apron wound.
She from a mother's anguish pours out cries,
Bends o'er her infant where entombed it lies,
Its calm cheek moistens from her tender eyes,
Its pale lips kisses o'er and o'er and o'er,
And deeper sobs with each long last *once more*,
Till Rodney's kindly touch she feels implore;
Then murmurs "good-bye, good-bye, mamma's May!"
And with a loud wail tears her wounded heart away.

Here sadness ends,
A new sun lends
His beams to light our way,
And pleasant sights,
And fair delights
Unite to raise our lay.
Where Freedom is what Freedom means,
Our lovers pass to other scenes.

Sussex Vale, Canada

Sweet vale of the Sussex! the pride of the Queen,
Whose life has a reign of beneficence been;
The flow'r of Britana's possessions afar
In the cold land, that lies beneath the North star.
No slaveholder's foot e'er polluted thy soil,
No slave in thy fields ever bended to toil.
As Bunyan's poor Christian who, fleeing for life,
Left the land of Destruction, and children and wife,
And saw as the shadow of Calv'ry he crost,
His burden rolled down and forever was lost;
So, when the poor fugitive, foot-sore and wan,
From the land of oppressors for liberty ran;
He found that his shackles would crumble and fall,
As he stood in the shadow of proud Montreal.

Asylum, fair Sussex, art thou of the free,
And of all the oppressed, that to thy arms flee
From "the land of the free, and home of the brave"—
Ah! land of the bound and the hell of the slave.

O, Sussex! dear Sussex! the scenes I remember,
As down thee I wander'd in yellow September!
The gay tinted woods in the sunset's gold gleaming,
The creek down thy midst like a sheet of light streaming,
The busy mill near it, and brown barns above,

And blithe childhood shouting in the deep still grove;
The lowing of herds, and the milkmaid calling;
And the tinkling of folds thro' the twilight falling.

And lo! a neat cottage with windows of green,
Scarce thro' the thick boughs of yon elms is seen!
There now the free lovers, that once were the slave,
The maid of the rice swamp and Rodney the brave,
Are dwelling in wedlock's dear holiest ties,
The objects of comment and pride for all eyes.

The stranger who passes thro' Sussex must hear
On the lips of the cottager, far and near,
The *love* of these new comers pointedly told,
And telling it over, it never grows old.

THE LITTLE GREEN COTTAGE

Canadian farmers came oft to the little green cottage,
To see their new neighbors and hear them tell over their troubles.
The tales of their pilgrimage e'er to their hearers had new charms;
And instances, once told, cloyed not in repeating them over.

Thus it was that farmers, as rough as the oaks in their forests,
But open, and clever, and frank as the brooks in their meadows,
Came oft in the twilight and sat in the door of the cottage,
And said: "We would hear of the land of the poor sable bondman."
And forward they leant, and sat mute as they heard the dark stories
That sully the brow of America's proudest endeavors.
And regarding Leeona with pity, they sighed: "Lord have mercy;"
As her words, soft and tender, fell on their great hearts with sweet
    pathos.
With wonder they look'd as they heard of the bayou and cane-brake;
Their breasts smote and murmured to hear of poor fugitive mothers

Chased down by fell bloodhounds, and dragged from the cypress
    swamps bleeding.
And their faces flamed red, and they plucked their long beard for
    resentment,
To hear of slave-holders who bought pure beauty and defiled it;
Blighting the hopes of the sweetest, the fairest, and youngest;
Adorning their harems with flowers all ruined but lovely!
And wringing from hoar age's heart submission to these vile abuses.
But they raised their broad hats, and shouted and stamped with
    boist'rous gladness,
To hear of Leeona escaping with Rodney her lover.

Thus it was that many an evening Rodney's friends came around him,
And far went the fame of the heroine of the savannas.
The same brave Rodney whose blows were too hard for the savage;
Whose feet were too swift, and whose arms were too strong for the
    bloodhound,
In his secret heart felt his whole life's fairest triumph
When he saw his Leeona the pride of all the great farmers.

Certain was he in his poverty and humble endeavors;
His little green cottage, tho' lowly, had its attractions—
Leeona, the womanly model of gentleness lived there.
Not young was she now, and radiant as she was aforetime,

Not thoughtlessly shy and blushing with reluctance so fawnlike,
Her arms were not smooth and round as they once were; her cheeks
    not so ruddy;
Her eyes were not so brilliant, and playful, and winning;
But softened by love, they beamed steadier and overcame more.
They were not the first stars that peep shyly thro' the whisp'ring twilight,
But the last sober-beaming ones that patiently linger
Above the familiar wood that watches the homes of our childhood.
She was not the bright light that once dazzled and charmed with its
    brilliance;
But settled and modest, the amiable light of the hearth-stone,
That draws all close about it, and sets all near hearts a chirping.

The wife of a good man, content to be his and to love him,
Ambitious to rival herself in his strong affections,
And ready always to lay hold with her hands and be happy.
A good wife was she, and loved all who loved her good husband;
And ever was ready to set him in the eyes of her friends
By kindness. Thus was she the idol of Rodney *and* his friends.

Not least among those who frequented the little green cottage
Was Father Eppinck, the good priest of the parish of Sussex.
A great and good man was he, and a true shepherd to all of his fold.
Were any by poverty shorn of the comforts of this life,
His mantle of care he threw around them, with love warmed.
Were the young gone astray in the dangerous wastes of transgression,
He followed their way, and returned with them prest to his bosom,
Were the old with woes pregnant, and burdened with great
    tribulations,
He led them, and gently pointed them to a more blessed future.
Thus it was that he came to the home of Leeona and Rodney,
With treasures of kind words. He called them his two loving children,
And always on leaving, he left them his best benediction.
He too loved Leeona, and came to hear of her pilgrimage.

                        A.A. WHITMAN

'Twas a balmy afternoon in the joyous vale of the Sussex,
And the voices of Autumn were heard in all of the north land.
The fields were shorn of their harvests, and the golden sheaves were
    gathered in,
And stacked in the barn-yards. The mill complained in the valley,

The distant glen echoed and sang with the music of axes,
And the wain came down from the deep woods groaning beneath its
    logs.
The forests wore gay colors, but sighed and were melancholy.
Then Father Eppinck, as he sate in the door of the cottage,
Lifted up his eyes and beheld the fair vale of the Sussex.
He saw the sweet tokens of peace that appeared in the heavens;
And he heard the voice of contentment that went up from the earth
    beneath;
The sweet words of plenty he heard, and the loud shouts of strong
    health;
And then he raised his voice and said: "O my God, I bless Thee!
For the rolling seasons and the full year, I magnify thee!
I thank thee for the hills and the high rock, and the great forests.
I thank thee for the pleasant valleys and their full fields of grain,
For their flowing streams, and the burdened orchards on their green
    banks.
I thank thee for plenty, for health, and for homes; but, oh my God!
I extol thee for freedom, the hope of the church of the Savior.
Here peace spreads her white wings, and sun never looks on a
    bondman.

Here earth yields her increase, and no slave's sweat ever falls upon it.
Oh God I bless thee for Canada and the Crown of England!"

When Father Eppinck had finished this saying, with kind words
He turned to Leeona and Rodney and said: "Now I leave you.
I go up to Montreal by the first coach to-morrow.
If the morning be fair, I hope to be off before cock crow.
A month shall I be gone, and now that the Autumn is far spent,
My coming to Sussex again will be in the Winter.
What time I am in Montreal, I will be in the house of a merchant,
A good man, whose wealth has kept pace with his increasing goodness;

A Christian, whose devotion to Christ and his holy Apostles
In alms deeds is shown. Samaritan-like he goes forward
Into the highways of this life, and gathers up the wounded
Spirit, and bears him in the arms of his wealth to the inn of comfort;
And when nakedness cries in the street, he hears her, and lends her
    help,
And asks not; 'But why are you naked? Why did you not save in
    harvest?'

And his lovely wife, the center of Montreal circles,

A brave hearted, noble, merciful and fair life consort,
Throws around him the arms of encouragement in all his good deeds.
She is happiest always among those that her hands have made happy.
Her heart is a fountain of kind words, and like Aquila of old,
She delights in the church of God, in Christ and his holy Apostles.
Her accomplishments drag after her a train of admirers;
Her beauty a train of worshippers, her charity a host
Of grateful lovers; while her affectionate fidelity
Lights up her home so that her husband says: 'A star is Dora.'"

Now Rodney hung his head when this last word, Dora, fell on his
    ears;
And as he bade Father Eppinck adieu, he looked up and sighed;
And the light of recollections flashed across his manly face
Like a burst of sun that thro' white clouds lights waving harvests.

One Snowy Night

The laughter of sleigh bells was heard on the lips of the snow storm
All day long, and passers were scarcely seen thro' the falling flakes
Hurriedly going, wrapped close, and one not speaking to another.
'Twas bitter cold, and the stiffened forests tossed in the northern blast;
And the great old pines, as the gale smote their snowy heads,
    grumbled,
And seemed in their anguish to mutter: "Let loose our hair and our
    whiskers!"
The slow wreathes of smoke curled dreamily thro' the still branches
That burdened with snow, stooped down and were sad-hearted and
    silent.
All sounds of the barn-yard were hushed in the chill breath of Winter.
The cottage was still, and within doors the cotter kept quiet.

The nightfall came, and still the flakes were coming thickly down.
"How it snows," said Leeona, as she shut the neat door of her cottage.

Then she drew her chair near Rodney, and sat before a a warm fire of
    logs.
This night the little green cottage was unusually cozy;
The cat on the rug sung low to the slumbering puppy,
Who yelped in a dream, and nipped at the heels of a rabbit.
The light of the fire-place, streaming across the clean hearth,
Glared on the walls, and flashed from the chairs and the tables,
Like the recollections of childhood flinging their cheer across life's path.

Now thus to her lord spoke the heroine of the Savannas:
"The approaching Christmas throws the shadows of mirth into Sussex.
Never before was there such buying of presents among us;
Never before such love without dissimulation."

Of a sudden Leeona hushed and fixed her eyes upon Rodney.
"Whoa!" cried a voice at the door, as rough as the oaths of a seaman,
"Still, Sorrel!" and a sleigh had stopped at the door of the cottage.
Leeona rose up quickly, but Rodney sat still and listened
Till she had opened the door and looked out in the darkness.

A dim lamp in the driver's hand streamed thro' the falling flakes
And discovered two men in the sleigh and one woman.
The men in their great coats wrapped dismounted, and then the
    woman,
Muffled in heavy furs, and veiled, stepped down between them;
When the driver reined his horses and dashed away in the silence.
The strangers entered the door and Father Eppinck before them,
And bowing, he said: "These are my friends of whom I spoke
    aforetime."

Rodney arose and stood erect in speechless wonder and silence,
As the tall and lovely form of Dora, the heroine of Saville,
Stood in the midst of the floor of his humble dwelling, and reached
The white hand of recognition, saying, with the sweetness of other
    days
"Do mine eyes behold thee, oh Rodney, my dearest benefactor!
I have heard of you here and have come to remove you to Montreal.
My home is a home for you, and the days of your toil are ended."

For the tears of gladness and gratitude the manly hero
Of a thousand trials hard could not speak, but he seized the small
    hand
Extended, and wept a benediction of tears upon it, and kissed it.
His great stern face of simple fidelity and manhood brave,
Was now lighted up with a glow exceeding portrayal,
And in its effulgence approaching those who stand in white robes
Ever, within the tidal glory of the Throne Eternal.
There were greetings then, and the joy of all hearts was running over;
And there countenances all shone with the light of the Kingdom of
    Heaven.

The End of the Whole Matter

A tall brave man of gray three score,
The sable columns rode before,
The knightliest of the knightly throng,
The bravest of the brave and strong
Who on the field of Nashville stood
Against the hosts of gallant Hood;
When noble Thomas, mild and brave,
Against the armed master, threw the former slave.

Rodney had left his home in foreign lands,
And laid his life into our country's hands,
His struggling kindred's conquests proud to share,
For he beheld acknowledged manhood there.
And this the grandest day that ever rose
Upon his life, at its eventful close
Was bringing with it recollections sweet,
That made his old heroic heart with youth's emotions beat

His country's banner, soiled and battle-torn,
In sable hands before the columns borne,
Streamed in the setting sun's deep golden light,
And rivaled Heaven in her blazon bright.
The drums of victory clamored on his ear;
The bugle's wail of rest was ringing clear,
Thunder of wheels was in the distance roaring,

And into camp the weary victors pouring.
He saw that Slav'ry's days were numbered now,
Far death's cold damp hung on her pallid brow.

And looking now upon his left and right,
Two proud sons who had ridden thro' the fight
With him, rode there with martial mien and brave,
The off'rings which Leeona's bosom gave
The country that had chased her as a slave.
He saw his sons, and prouder felt than he
Who took Rebellion's sword from famous Lee.

This was the day when Southern chivalry
Beheld black manhood clothed in liberty,
Step from the shadow of his centuries
Of bondage, shake dejection from his eyes,
And to the awful verge of valor rise.
The day that heard the negro, scarred and maimed,
On sovereign battle's lips a man proclaimed.

The hosts of Sherman marching to the sea,
Beneath Rebellion's trembling canopy
Swept like a thunder storm, whose lightnings catch
The shaking hills with hands of flame, and snatch
Their mighty forests down. The Nation then
Lifted her hands to Heaven and praised the men
Who cleaved their way by hard incessant blows,
From where the hills of Cumberland arose,
And at the Northern door of Slavedom held

Their watch, to where the Mexic Ocean swelled;
Wrenching fair victory from brave hands and true
As e'er on foe the steel of battle drew,
The Alpine strength of strongholds sweeping down,
And treading under foot each hostile town.
Then fair applause warmed her white hands with claps,
And bright-faced greetings at all doors gave raps,
Gray bearded gratitude bowed on his knees,
And cheering cities flamed with jubilees.

But soon a change came o'er the Nation's face,
The light of mirth to clouds of fear gave place.
The chiming bells that jubilantic rung,
Now hushed their throats or spoke with doleful tongue.
The mazy dance held her light-booted feet,
And music soft suppressed her murmurs sweet.
Sad-faced religion sought the church once more,
And faith went back to do her first works o'er.

The gallant Hood, intrepid Sherman knew
Would cleave the Slaveholder's domains in two,

So, as that military comet went
To Southward, he his swift flight Northward bent.
The Union struck at proud Rebellion's heart;
Rebellion aimed at her same vital part,
And doubtless had a wound most painful made,
Had not the Union's negro arm displayed
Such valiant strength in warding off the blow,
And striking down the strong and gallant foe.

As Rodney rode to camp this glorious day,
He heard a dying soldier by his way,
Half hidden 'mong his mangled comrades pray.
His tortured soul of ruin conscious cried,
Raved thro' its mansion dark from side to side,
Rose to the eyes. and stood with dreadful glare,
Ran to the heart, and fluttered, groaning there,
And shuddering in the awful shades of woe,
Sank down in mortal dread and pleaded not to go.
As hope forever bade her host farewell,
Now mem'ry came into the soul's dark cell,
And with the wrongs of unrepented yore,
Manacled her, and chained her to the floor.
Remorse then followed with the criminal's scourge,
Her pris'ner seized, and dragged towards the verge
Of mis'ry bottomless, and 'mid the smoke
Of black torment, that rolled and spread and broke,
Laid on her lash of scorpions with heavy stroke.

"Oh, Lord!" the sufferer cries, "have mercy now!
I would pray right, Lord Jesus, teach me how!
Ah! I've insulted thee, I know, I own,
But Savior, make thy boundless mercies known;
Oh, life misspent, could I but now recall!
Leeona, Rodney, ah! forgive me all.
Help! water! water! water, or I die!"
"Who's here?" cries Rodney, quickly turning by,
The dying man stares on the speaker brave,

In ghastly silence, as the whisper "save!"
Falls from his lips; then like a madman yells,
And rolls his painful balls within their fevered cells.

Rodney forgets the wrongs of other years,
As wretchedness' bitter cry he hears;
The red wounds that with parched lips appeal
To heav'n he sees, and can't his tears conceal.
He kneels upon the ground where Aylor lies,
His canteen to his quiv'ring lips applies,
The sinking body in his arms doth rest,
And leans his throbing head against his breast.
Now stooping o'er, the hero hears the cry:
"Rodney, I know, forgive me ere I die!
Leeona tell"—he fixes here his eyes,
And still in death, on Rodney's bosom lies.

And now my country let us bury all
Our blunders sad beneath grim battle's pall.
Gathered beneath the storm's heroic folds,
While our dear land an aching bosom holds,
Let us forget the wrongs of blue and grey,
In gazing on the grandeur of the fray.
Now let the vanquished his repentant face,
Lean in the victor's merciful embrace,
And let the victor, with his strong arm heal
The bleeding wounds that gape beneath his steel.
And may no partial hand attempt a lay

Of praise, as due alone to blue or grey.
The warrior's wreath may well by both be worn,
For braver man than either ne'er was born.
They both have marched to death and victory,
They both have shown heroic misery,
And won the soldier's immortality.
But scars of honor that they both yet wear,
The proudest testimonials of their valor are.

And where our sons their battle lances drew,
Fought not their sable comrades bravely too?
Let Wagner answer 'mid the reeking storm,
That mingles with black dead proud Shaw's fair form.
Ask it of Fisher, and a thousand more
Brave fields that answer with their lips of gore.
And while America's escutcheon bright,
Is bathed in war-won Freedom's glorious light,
Forget it not, the colored man will fight.
More patriotism Sparta never knew,
A lance more knightly Norman never threw,
More courage never armed the Roman coasts,
With blinder zeal ne'er rode the Moslem hosts,
And ne'er more stubborn stood the Muscovite,
Than stood the hated negro in the fight.

The war was God-sent, for the battle blade,
Around the seething gangrene, Slavery, laid,
By Heaven's arm, this side and that was prest,

Until the galling shame dropt from the Nation's breast.
War was inevitable, for the crimes
That stained our hands (and in the olden times
Engendered) now were Constitutional,
And spreading thro' the Nation's body all.
Deep rooted where the vital currents meet
Around the heart of government, their seat
Evaded Legislation's keenest skill,
Or bent the stoutest edge of human will.
'Twas then that God the raving Nation threw
Upon her own war lance and from her drew,
By accidental providence, a flood
Of old diseases that lurked in her blood.

Whom Moses witnessed 'mid old Sinai's smoke,
Whose arm from Judah's neck had torn the yoke,
And with it broken Egypt's bones of pride,
And with his chariots strown the Red Sea tide;
Who stripped the golden crimes from Babel's throne,

And made his pow'r to Baal's adorers known;
He stood among us and His right arm bared
To show His ways by seers of old declared.
While millions trembled at Oppression's nod,
Oppression sank beneath the finger touch of God.
Line upon line the centuries had wrought,
And precept upon precept vainly taught,
The prophets had of old been heard to cry,
While signs and wonders figured in the sky,

And then the Incarnation of all good,
By Jordan's wave and in the Mount had stood,
And with His hand of gentleness and love
Transcendent, that a heart of stone could move,
Had touched the ties of every human woe,
And loosing fettered mind, said: "Let him go."
And His great heart to patience ever moved,
And always gentle e'en if He reproved,
Bore this sweet sentence from his sinless Home:
"To preach deliv'rance to the bound I'm come."
But even then, our country shook her head,
Her eagle wings of independence spread,
One tipped with fires of the Tropic's glow,
The other lashing in the realms of snow,
And in her pride declared that God's own Son
Had licensed Slavery's dark crimes, every one.
And tho' we shackled Afric's sable hands,
And scourged her where the smoking altar stands,
And tho' we loaded down her captive feet
With iron chains, right by the mercy seat,
And tho' we laid her virgin bosom bare,
And forced her where the fires of off'ring glare;
We smote our conscience with a palm of ease,
And thanked God that his pure eye ever sees!
Who then can wonder that the Lord would smite
The haughty neck that did Him thus despite?

Now let us in the light of future years,

Forget our loss and sacrificial tears,
And thank kind heav'n that tho' we erred and strayed,
We to the good path our return have made.

Hail dawning Peace! Speed on thy glorious rise!
And with thy beams unseal the nation's eyes.
Let Islam in the blaze of scimitar
Proclaim his rites, and gorge the fangs of war,
But peace be unto thee, land of our sires,
Whose sacred altar flames with holier fires!
Let lawlessness no longer stagger forth
With his destructive torch, nor South nor North;
And let the humblest tenant of the fields,
Secured of what his honest labor yields,
Pursue his calling, ply his daily care,
His home adorn and helpless children rear,
Assured that while our flag above him flies,
No lawless hand can dare molest his joys.

Lo! from yon hights, land of the rising star,
The hands of Freedom beckon from afar,
And mid the glad acclaims of roused mankind
Fling her immortal standard to the wind;
Speed there thy flight, and lead the glorious train
That swell the lofty tributes of her reign.
Thy hands are wrested from the tyrant's hold,

Thy name on Time's illustrious page enrolled,
And thy escutcheon bright, embossed with gold.

From Erie's rock-watched shores to Mexic's sands,
No more the bondman wrings his fettered hands;
No more entreaty's sable face thro' tears,
Looks on for succor thro' the weary years;
For Freedom's holy dawn is now begun,
And earth rejoices 'neath her rising sun.
Requited toil content pursues his care,
Walks with bold strides as free as heaven's air;
The gen'rous fields put on their aspect sweet,

And forests blithe their hymns of God repeat.
Dear western woods! thou harbors of the free,
With youthful hearts we wander back to thee,
And ere these numbers hush, once more would lie
Beneath thee stretched and gaze upon the sky.
Thou art more proud than Windsor's lofty shade,
By poet sung, or by the sage portrayed.
No lordly despot o'er thy ample grounds,
Sways ancient titles and proclaims his bounds;
But each poor tenant *owns* his humble plot,
Tills his neat farm and rears his friendly cot.
The weary trav'ler 'long thy roads may lie,
As peaceful as the brook that rambles by,
From boughs that drop with plenty gather food,
And o'er his dear ones rear a shelter rude.
Thou noble seats! fit theme of bard or sage,

Beneath thy bow'rs leans venerable age,
While from the summit of his stalwart years,
His life's calm twilight slowly disappears,
And hope's sweet sunrise in the future nears.
And where smooth paths thy solemn shades divide,
Walks buoyant toil with young love at his side,
And charmed by songs that ev'ry zephyr shakes
From boughs around, his hopeful journey takes.
And flaxen childhood there the live-long day,
In blithe sports whirls and wanders far away.

Oh comrade freemen strike your hands to stand
Like walls of rock and guard our father-land!
Oh guard our homes and institutions free,
The price of blood and valor's legacy.
Awake to watch, ye sovereign sons of toil!
If despot feet e're touch our country's soil,
Fly to the standard that by freemen born,
The glory of a hundred years has worn,
Blood-stained, yet bright, streaming, but battle-torn,
And *rally* till the last drop from the veins
Of free America flows on our plains.

Eternal vigilance must light the tower,
Whose granite strength can bide the evil hour,
Whose wave-dashed base defies the tempest's shock,
Builded upon the everlasting rock.
At last, proud land, let potent wisdom write
Her name above thy brow in glorious light,

And suffer ne'er thy hands to idle rest
Till learning lights thy humblest subject's breast.
In cities tall, and in the hamlet rude,
Suffer no partial hand to e'er exclude
A single poor from fair instruction's halls,
But write EQUALITY on all her walls.
An equal chance in life, and even start,
Give every one and let him play his part.
But who could, with complacence on his face,
First bind one's feet, then *challenge* for a race?
I would not own I was a thing so small,
I'd rather own I was no man at all,
Than show that I must some advantage take,
The race of life respectably to make.
Say my facilities must all be *best*,
Then write excelsior upon my crest?
Nay, rather let me weed the hardest row,
And rise above by *toiling* from below.

Free schools, free press, free speech and equal laws,
A common country and a common cause,
Are only worthy of a freeman's boasts—
Are Freedom's *real* and intrinsic costs.
Without these, Freedom is an empty name,
And war-worn glory is a glaring shame.
Soon where yon happy future now appears,
Where learning now her glorious temple rears,
Our country's hosts shall round one interest meet,

And her free heart with one proud impulse beat,
One common blood thro' her life's channels flow,
While one great speech her loyal tongue shall know.

And soon, whoever to our bourne shall come,
Jew, Greek or Goth, he here shall be at home.
Then Ign'rance shall forsake her crooked ways,
And poor old Caste there end her feeble days.

THE END

MISCELLANEOUS POEMS

PEACE

As the raindrop on a flower
When the bow's behind a shower,
As the breeze that fans the forehead
Of the sunset, when his cheeks red
Nestle on his mountain pillow,
Or a sea without a billow;
So is Peace's sweet libations,
To the bosom of the Nations.

While the Shepherd's lone were tending
Flocks by night on Judah's plain;
Angels bright above them bending,
Trumpeted their sweet refrain:

"Glory be to God in Heaven,
Peace on earth, good will to men,
To the world a Savior's given,
Lo! he comes in Bethlehem.

Then a door in Heaven opened,
And a milk-white spirit flew

From the golden portals earthward—
And the Nation's journeying thro',

She touched the Conqu'ror's Sword, that thrust
Thro' thousand hearts red honors wore;
The glitt'ring terror fell before
His eyes and crumbled into dust.

She breathed upon the warrior's wreath,
And while applauses filled his ears,
And earth her tribute paid of tears,
His glory withered in her breath.

She stood behind the tyrant's throne;
His sceptre vanished from his hand;

And lo! he saw on sea and land,
His gloomy power was gone.

She fanned the lab'rer's care-worn brow,
And sunshine falling from her wing
Into his heart, forced him to sing
While leaning on his plow.

Then by his cot she turned her flight,
And blithe health to the doorway ran,
Contentment's sweetest songs began,
And all within was light.

Hymn to the Nation

When Science, trembling in the lengthened shade
Of monster superstitions, and menaced
By raving Bigotry, a dream embraced
Of prosperous worlds by mortal unsurveyed,
Genoa's seaman and a daring few;
Wide Ocean's stormy perils rent and brought her bounds to view.

Who then had thought that with the Eternal mind,
That in vast Future's covered bosom bound—
Shut up—by these sea-roamers to be found,
Was this green home of poor, abused mankind,
This land of exiles, and the peaceful borne,
Where Babel's scattered tongues shall yet to one great speech return.

Fair Freedom travailed 'neath an unknown sky,
And tho' the tyrant shook his envious chain,
And tho' the bigot reared a gloomy fane,
She bore our darling of the azure eye;
Baptized its childhood in brave blood and tears,
But trumpted her independence in Great Britian's ears.

Astonished kingdoms heard of the new birth,
And royal vengeance drew her warring blade,
And bloody strokes upon Columbia laid,

To smite the young offender to the earth;
Colonial hardships shivered where she went,
And border horrors thro' the years a thrill of sadness sent.

But patriotism bold, sustained the blow,
Returning deeper wounds with daring might—
For Freedom ever steels the stroke of right—
And cool determined Valor's proud arm so
Dismayed the imperial hosts, that baffled George
Saw he could ne'er enslave the men who withstood Valley Forge.

A century has spun around the wheel
Of ages, and the years in noiseless flight
Have heaped their golden tributes to the right;
Till now religion in her heavenly zeal,
To mend life's ills walks hand in hand with lore,
Where clank the chains of slaves in Law's offended ears no more.

Here honest labor trembles at the nod
Of no despot; and penury no more
Must with her gaunt and withered arm implore
Scant life, at Charity's closed hands; but God
Doth lead the bounteous thousands as a flock,
And Peace's happy voices echo from the Nation's Rock.

Tho' at the name Republic tyrants mocked,
Columbia has lived a hundred years

Thro' trials, triumphs, hopes, and doubts and fears,
And still she lives, tho' often tempest-rocked,
Republic yet, united, one and free,
And may she live; her name the synonyme of Liberty!

Go forth ye children of the valiant land,
Go, sound the timbrel of her praises loud!
Ye Alleghenies, in your ascent proud
Thro' cloud-surrounded realms, the winds command
That revel in your soaring locks, to raise
One harmony, and mingle all their hoarsest notes in praise!

Ye Rocky mountains, as with awful glee,
Or icy scorn, ye stare against the sun
Whose shafts glance harmless your strong front upon,
And splintered fall, awake the Western Sea
To join the thunders of your snowy reign,
And speak responsive to your neighbors tow'ring o'er the plain!

Stride on, thou dread Niagara, stride on!
Thou lord of waters, in thy mighty wrath,
And thy earth rocking leap into the bath

Of thunders, stride on! Omnipotent, alone!
And from thy stony lungs her praises sound,
Till Mexic's potent Sea reply and Oceans shout around!

The Lute of Afric's Tribe

To the memory of Dr. J. McSimpson, a colored Author of Anti-Slavery
Ballads. Written for the Zanesville, O., Courier.

When Israel sate by Babel's stream and wept,
The heathen said, "Sing one of Zion's songs;"
But tuneless lay the lyre of those who slept
Where Sharon bloomed and Oreb vigil kept;
For holy song to holy ears belongs.

So, when her iron clutch the Slave power reached,
And sable generations captive held;
When Wrong the gospel of endurance preached;
The lute of Afric's tribe, tho' oft beseeched,
In all its wild, sweet warblings never swelled.

And yet when Freedom's lispings o'er it stole,
Soft as the breath of undefiled morn,
A wand'ring accent from its strings would stroll—
Thus was our Simpson, man of song and soul,
And stalwart energies, to bless us born.

When all our nation's sky was overcast
With rayless clouds of deepening misery,
His soaring vision mounted thro' the blast,
And from behind its gloom approaching fast,
Beheld the glorious Sun of Liberty.

He sang exultant: "Let her banner wave!"
And cheering senates, fired by his zeal,
Helped snatch their country from rebellion's grave
Looked through brave tears upon the injured slave,
And raised the battle-arm to break his gyves of steel.

But hushed the bard, his harp no longer sings
The woes and longings of a shackled mind;
For death's cold fingers swept its trembling strings,

And shut the bosom of its murmurings
Forever on the hearing of mankind.

The bird that dips his flight in noonday sun,
May fall, and spread his plumage on the plain;
But when immortal mind its work hath done
On earth, in heaven a nobler work's begun,
And it can never downward turn again.

Of him, whose harp then, lies by death unstrung—
A harp that long his lowly brethren cheered,
May'nt we now say, that, sainted choirs among,
An everlasting theme inspires his tongue,
Where slaves ne'er groan, and death is never feared?

Yes, he is harping on the "Sea of glass,"
Where saints begin, and angels join the strain;
While Spheres in one profound, eternal bass,
Sing thro' their orbs, illumined as they pass,
And constellations catch the long refrain.

To the Student

Who flees the regions of the lower mind,
Where these distempers breathe on every wind:
Infectious dogmatisms, noxious hate,
Old snarly spleen, and troublesome debate,
Dull bigotry, and stupid ignorance,
Proud egotism, empty arrogance,
And famous hollowness, and brilliant woe—
And would to knowledge's high places go,
Must first in humble prayer approach the Throne
Of the Almighty Mind, and there make known
The purposes that swell an honest heart;
Then on the path before him, meekly start:
Asking of others who have been that way,
What of the country, and what of the day?
Being certain ever to give earnest heed
To where the steps of hoar experience lead.
Mark him who ventures these means to despise,
And tho' his works in gloomy grandeur rise,
Awe strike all earth, and threaten e'en the skies;
Yea, "tho' he flourish like a green bay tree,"
His life will a stupendous (stupeduous) failure be.
Tis vain to soar aloft on borrowed wing,
Or drink success from favor's flowing spring.
Let him who journeys upward, *learn* the way,

By toiling step by step, and day by day.
Each hardship mounted, easier makes the next,
And leaves his pathway by one less perplext.
Lo! where yon dreamer looks on glory's hill,
Hopes to ascend without the manly *will*,
Bends round and round some open pass to try
With easy access, and ascend on high;
Waits for some helper till the day is past,
And night o'ertakes a sycophant at last.
But honest courage, see with manful strides,
Walks on and enters at the steepest sides,

Climbs long and slowly up his rugged path,
Awaits no aid, relies on what he hath,
Grows independent as his way proceeds,
As progress roughens, less the distance heeds,
Till lo! the utmost hights his footsteps meet,
With fames and fortunes lying at his feet.
Then Kings delight to honor Glory's son,
And loud applauses in his footsteps run.
Then mankind crave the favor of his eyes,
And heap his lasting tributes to the skies.

Written for the Zanesville (O.,) Courier.

CUSTAR'S LAST RIDE

Forth on the fatal morn,
Proud as the waves of Horn
Rode the cavalier;
Followed by gallant men,
Far in a rocky glen
To disappear.

"Halt!" bands of Sioux are seen
O'er all the dark raine,
Crouched in numbers vast;
"Halt!" and a hush, "Prepare!"
"Charge!" and the very air
Starts at the blast.

Long waves of horsemen break,
And hoofy thunders wake
On the steep glen sides.
Back roll the columns brave,
Back in a smoky grave,
Each hero rides.

"Ready!" their chieftain cries,
Steady his eagle eyes
Sweep the dark ground o'er.
Slowly the lines re-form,

Slowly returns the storm,
Yet dreadful more.

"Charge!" is the proud command,
Onward the daring band
Like a torrent dash;
On heaving gorges long,
On groaning rocks among,
With tempest crash.

Up from their ferny beds
Dart fields of pluming heads,
As if hideous earth,
Out of her rocky womb,
Out of an army's tomb,
Doth give them birth.

"Rally!" but once is heard,
"Rally!" and not a word,
The brave boys rallying, speak.
Lightnings of valiant steel
Flash fast; the columns reel,
Bend—reel and break!

"Stand!" cries their Custar proud,
"Stand!" in the battle cloud
Echoes high around.
Answers the sabre's stroke,
Tho' in black waves of smoke
His fair form 's drown'd.

Firece hordes of painted braves
Melt down, for well behave
Horse and cavalier:
As round their chief they fall,
Cheered by his clarion call,
From front to rear.

No more their leader calls,
Pierced 'mid his men he falls,
But sinks breathing, "Stand!"
And where the hero lies,
Each soldier till he dies,
Fights hand to hand.

SONNET.—THE MONTENEGRIN

Undaunted watcher of the mountain track,
Tho' surging cohorts like a sea below,
Against thy cliff-walled homes their thunders throw;
Proud, whilst thy rocky fastness answers back
The fierce, long menace of the Turk's attack,
Thy eagle ken above the tumult flies,

The hostile plain spurns, and its prowess black,
And lights on strongholds terraced in the skies;
There thou wilt quicker than the roe-buck bound,
If bolder dangers mount to force thy pass;
But not till thou a signal brave hast wound,
That hears responses from each peak around,
And calls thy comrade clans-in-arms, to mass
In high defence, when battle stern begins—
Then who can conquer the Montenegrins?

Solon Stiles. Humorous

To town one day rode Solon Stiles,
O'er weary roads and rocky miles,
And thro' long lanes, whose dusty breath,
Did nearly smother him to death;
By ragged fences, old and brown,
And thro' great tall woods up and down.

Wide orchards robed in red and white,
Were singing on his left and right;
The forests carroled by his way,
The grass was chirping, green and gay,
And wild flow'rs, sweetest of their race,

Like country maids of bashful face,
Peeped thro' the briery fences nigh,
With bright hues in each timid eye.
The farm cows whisked in their cool nook,
And splashed within their peaceful brook;
And on his fence, beneath the shade,
The plow boy's pipe shrill music made.

Stiles saw all this, but what cared he,
When he was going the town to see?
The country he had always seen,
But into town had never been.
So on he rode, with head on high,
And great thoughts roaming thro' the sky,
Not caring what he trotted by.

A little mule he sat astride,
With ropes for stirrups o'er him tied,
In which huge boots, as red as clay—
Red as a fox, some folks would say—
Swung loosely down, and dangled round,
As if in hopeless search of ground.

At first, when from the woods he rode,
And high in sight his small mule trode,
Rough seas of smoke rolled on his eye,
Great dizzy houses reared on high,
With steeples banging in the sky,
Then Solon stopped and said, "Umph, my!"

And next, a river deep and wide,
With houses floating *up* its tide
He met, and paused again to look,
And then to move on undertook.
And spurred and spurred, but looked around,
And lo! in deep amazement found
His small mule stuck, and as he spurred
The more, the thing's ears only stirred.
"Hullo!" a swarm of blubbies cried,
"Whip on the critter's hairy side!"
At this the mule insulted grew,
Took up its ears, and fairly flew,
Till near a great white bride it drew.

Across the bridge rode Solon Stiles,
By dusty shops and lumber piles,
And where tall houses o'er him stood,
Like cliffs within his native wood.
And furnaces with firey tongues,
And smoky throats and iron lungs,
Like demons coughed, and howled, and roared,
And fire from out their bowels poured.

Now on and on, up Sailor street,
The donkey whirled his rattling feet,
While either sidewalk loud upon
A swarm of oaths were chorused on.
One tall boy, in this surging sea

Of rags and young profanity,
High o'er the rest, on awkward shanks,
Like stilts, led on the swelling ranks.

A.A. WHITMAN

His deep throat like a fog horn blew,
Till lesser blasts their aid withdrew.

Then Stiles communed thus with his mule:
"My! listen what a cussin' school
This town lets out to fill the ears
Of God with! My! them babies swears!"
Meanwhile there came a light brigade,
To at the donkey's heels parade,
Till up before and then behind,
His honor flew and then combined,
An old Dutch waltz and new quick-step,
That half a square of urchins swept,
As fast as leaves were ever seen,
Brushed by a whirlwind from the green.

The tall commander now in front,
Led oathing, as his pride was wont,
The new assault, when stock still stood
The mule away not half a rood;
For lo! with tomahawk in hand,
Before a neighb'ring cigar stand,
He saw a savage; to describe
A chieftain of some bloody tribe.
At Solon straight he raised a blow

And strained with all his might to throw,
But stayed his rage, for he beheld,
That with hot rage the donkey swelled.

Ah! Solon felt his blood run cold,
For oft his gran'dad him had told
Of Indians in an early day,
Beside the bockwoods cotter's way,
Skulking to on some settler fly,
And scalp him ere he'd time to die.
"Throw if you dare!" aloud he cried,
And slid down at his donkey's side.
At this he saw the savage stare,

And forthwith threw his coat off there.
With club in hand, the first he found,
Then on the foe at one great bound
He flew, and hard began to pound;
When thus abroad-brimmed vender fat,
Began to interview the spat:
"Vat vas-yer dun, yer grazy ding;
Schoost schtop, yer petter don't py jing!
Schoost vat yer broke my zine mit, aye,
Eh! petter yer don't, yer go avay!"

"Well!" Solon thought, "If this is town,
I'll give you leave to knock me down
If I ain't lost; no, this ain't me,

No, town ain't what it seems to be,
Yes, here I am, and this is me,
But town's not what it seems to be!"

THE THUNDER STORM

Lo! how the Heavens ponder now,
They look so still and moody!
And every leaf, and every bough,
Are in a dark deep study.

The very air has hushed its breath,
And pauses in its hushing,
To hear the clouds that still as death,
Are out of darkness rushing.

The lightnings in their vivid wrath,
The waving hills a starting,
Deep thro' the cloud-sea cleave a path,
From shore to shore a darting,

Loud thunders roll within the flood,
And night peers on with wonder,
And seems to sigh, in pensive mood,
And whisper, "hear it thunder!"

Again the thunders shriek aloud,
Far o'er the distance roaring,
And now from every breaking cloud,
The sluicy floods are pouring.

Upon the roof, the dancing drops
Come down with splash and clatter,
The lightnings glare, their music stops—
Now louder 'gins to patter;

As if to catch its breath, the rain
Were, when it thundered, pausing,
Then rushing on to make again
The time it had been losing.

To Baby's Canary, Accidentally Killed

Thou tiny cheer,
So welcome wast thou here,
Coming to our home with baby bright,
To make our hearts glad, and our burdens light;
We hoped that thou and he
Would merry playmates be.

Thy voice, sweet bird,
And baby's chirp we heard,
But only knew that both must happy be,
But how much happier were both, thought we,
If thou wast older grown,
And baby thee had known!

Now baby sweet,
Looks at thy little feet,
And holds thy fallen plume in his wee hands;
Thy mournful fate, it seems he understands.
Oh! we are sad to see
Him gaze at us—then thee!

THE DESERTED ROAD

Away thro' the blue distant hills,
Thou windest, deserted old Road;
By farm houses brown and gray mills
And log huts, the woodman's abode.

Since enterprise with iron speed,
Steams on over mountain and plain,
Industry of thee hath no need,
And leaves thee washed red by the rain.

But such was not always the case,
For yonder where wanes the ago,
Loud Travel with bright, hopeful face,
Rolled over thee proudly but slow.

Then rudeness with plenty was blest,
And health was the consort of toil;
Then "far as the East from the West,"
Was business from panic's turmoil.

But fast times have lured with great shows,
The simple from certainty's shore,
To where wealth into wealth *only* flows,
And scorns the bare hands of the poor.

Alas! since we all can't be rich,
Allow the poor poverty's ways;
Contentment will bring all that which
Wealth finds in her wasteful displays.

The orbit too great for the sphere,
Speeds motion too fast or too slow;
Let poverty learn to dwell where
Fair Plentitude's hilltops are low.

Ambition deceives with a smile,
Those who in the gust of the times,

Instead of the sure calm of toil,
Would rush into wealth-blooming climes.

To speed on thro' life's a mistake,
To reach our desires too soon;
The charm of expecting will break,
And bring on our night before noon.

Our pleasures reaped singly are best,
More lasting by far gathered slow;
The fields in sweet flowers are drest,
That come in their seasons—then grow.

The many old pleasures that die,
Make but the sparse new that remain,
Which none but proud fortune can buy,
While nothing the poor can retain.

We want on the wasting old Road,
To wake dusty travel once more,
To people each wayside abode,
And drive business up to each door.

Written for the Zanesville (O.,) Courier.

A.A. WHITMAN

Old Abe, the War Eagle of Wisconsin

Heard ye of "Old Abe," the war eagle who went
From his home by the Lakes to the far sunny coasts,
To share the brave fortunes of that regiment
Which numbered the Eighth in Wisconsin's proud hosts?
When army clouds mingled in that civil storm
Which hung o'er the Nation in deep low'ring gloom,
Above a horizon of breastworks his form,
The emblem of Liberty, proudly did plume.

Away in the dimness of uncertain strife
He spread his bold flight towards Victory's sky—
Tho' treason smote hard at the National life—
And soared to her parapets looking on high.

From whence mangled Slavery, low at the feet
Of proud stamping battle, he stooped then to spurn,
And homeward flew back with the brave boys to meet
The loved ones who waited? wanted? (wainted) to hail their return.

Written for the Zanesville (O.,) Courier.

Prosperity and Adversity

When first the young year inhales the sweetened air,
And painted landscapes kiss her tender feet,
The constant throat of music everywhere
Is burdened with her meed of praises sweet.

The clear brook panting from the ivied steep,
A crystal tribute sings within the dell;
And in the branchy wood secluded deep
Soft echo marks the sounds that please her well.

Till blooming Summer drops her latest charms,
Contentment tunes her reed in labor's ear;
Till russet plenty crowns the joyous farms,
The tongue of greetings hails the jovial year.

But when the sullen North begins to wail,
Old friends forsake her, leaving one by one;
Till all untended in her leafless vale,
The naked year is left to die alone.

Then saddened blasts convey her snowy bier,
And only blustry storm above her weeps,
While mournful woods attempt a feeble cheer,
And cold drear suns but glance at where she sleeps.

Written for the Zanesville (O.,) Courier.

A Dream of Glory

True glory on the earth is seldom seen,
Tho' sought by many with a jealous eye;
For where the heavenly birth has ever been,
The heedless footsteps of the world pass by.

The fairest blooms are born of humble weeds,
That faint and perish in the pathless wood;
And out of bitter life grow noble deeds,
To pass unnoticed in the multitude.

But reared by care, within the garden neat,
Luxuriant chances beautify the whole;
While poison lurks beneath each painted sweet,
And shoots a sorrow thro' the admiring soul.

Poor homeless hearts, unpitied by mankind,
And fortunes shattered in the adverse blast,
Are signals that have marked the march of mind,
Through boasted civ'lization's glorious past.

The dauntless *will* that scorns threat'ning defeat,
And breaks thro' penury's strong prison bars;
Can plant on triumphs proud his tow'ring feet,
And walk a shining highway to the stars.

MORTON

Freedom, thy son is dead!
Once more the solemn tread
Of the long, slow cortege echoes to throbs
Of a nation's heart, and a great people's sobs
Around their leader's bier,
Burst on the sorrowing ear.
The lips of mirth are still,
And the eyes of beauty fill
With big tears;
The voice of love is low,
The hands of trade move slow,
And toil wears
A deep grief on his brow.
The tongues of sad bells cleaving
To the roofs of their mouths speak not;
And music's bosom heaving
Beneath its burden is silent.

Fair Indiana weeps,
The central mourner of a group of States,
That come with tears to shed
Around the mighty dead.
Alas! poor Indiana!
Too late in him who sleeps,
Thou see'st a noble son,
So soon "worn out" and done!
His voice is hushed forever in thy gates.
Alas! poor Indiana!
Now is a time for memory and tears,
And lessons that fall from the lips of years.
Sit down in the shadow that like a dark pall
From this sad event doth over thee fall,
With a hand on thy heart, and a hand on thy head,
And mourn the great loss in the glorious dead.
Thou hast sisters who may *with* thee mourn,
But *none for* thee, for none *thy* loss have borne.

Now is a time for reflection.
A star has gone down.
But the light that shone,
Yet lingers on our sight;
And we turn in the direction
In which we last saw it going,
And pensively pause, scarce knowing
That all around is night.

Weep for Indiana!
Ye her sisters who gave
Our flag an arm of help in peril's hour:
And raised the injured slave
From iron heeled oppression's galling power.
Weep, States, for Indiana!
Her Morton saved her, when she strove the awful leap
Into Rebellion's vortex dread to take.
The rocky jaws of ruin gaping deep
Beneath, began her head to dizzy make;
And wild hallucinations that did rise
From slavery's hell of wrongs had sealed her eyes
To danger; on the brink a moment, lost
To Freedom's sweet entreating voice, she tossed
Her tresses back, and in fair frenzy gazed
Upon our glorious flag; a mad cry raised,
And sprang for death; but seized by her great son,
Who to the awful rescue swift had run,
And forced in herculean arms away,
She mourns him, clothed in her right mind to-day.

Toll the bells for a nation's sorrow,
Toll slow, toll slow!
Chant songs of a people's sorrow,
Chant low, chant low.
Behold the great man borne
Towards the waiting tomb!
Open earth! Give him room!
Environed in the gloom
That lowers, mourn, people! mourn!

And with the solemn boom
Of cannon, and the knells
Of sad sorrowing bells,
Proclaim, proclaim his doom!

His glory was to *serve* his State—
She gave him none;—he was born great.
In his country's woe he found his own,
His weal in his country's weal,
Self in his great works never was known—
A patriot true as steel.
Born to rule, he knew the reins,
And knew the rod, and spared no pains
In using either, when they need be.
As restless as the uncontented sea,
He knew no stand still.
Stronger forever growing he
Was in *man will*.
He was the lion who could awe the weak
By lying still in massive dread reserve,
Or fly upon the strong opposer's neck
With scornful glare, and blows of iron nerve.
And sun ne'er looked upon a day,
Since our Republic tore away
Her arms from Britain's clutch,
That would not have seen him in *front*,
As in our times his life was wont;
The elements were such
In him, and so combined
Were all the powers of his vast mind.
His was no warrior's wreath—
He not on cannon's breath
O'er red fields rode to death
And immortality;
But strong for liberty
He rose in dreadful might—
Dreadful because of right—
And with the weapons bright
That genius gave her favorite son,

He dealt dismay and death to foes
Far mightier than those
Who dare the flash of steel and reeking gun.

When human slav'ry struggled to extend
Its snaky coil round California's coasts,
And thro' our trembling land from end to end,
Flaunting Secession made his open boasts,
He met the hissing wrong,
And cool, and brave, and strong,
Drove back its forked tongue.

When loyal heads hung down,
'Neath mad opinion's frown,
And tongues more fearful froze;
His was to oppose
With clearest words of stone,
Hewn from the loyal block,
Whose meaning always known,
With true energy thrown,
Smote like the rock.

When freedom's columns waved,
And friends of the enslaved
Aghast fell back,
His courage knew no lack—
He hurried to the van,
The thickest dangers braved,
And e'er the battle saved;
So nobly he behaved—
The cause lived in the man.
He could endure, rebuke, compel, entreat,
Forbear, defy, but could not know defeat.

First always in the right,
Doing with all his might,
And last to yield the fight,
His friends learned to depend upon him,
And his foes feared to rush upon him,

And both joined to wonder at him,
And slander ceased to thunder at him,
And envy ceased to sneak behind him,
And everywhere applause would find him,
Till rumor held her speech before him;
And now he's gone, we all adore him.

Two there were who fought
Our struggles dire;
One in the battle's hell,
Met by destruction's yell,
And the death rain of shot and shell,
For his country strove;
One the great work of love
With his mind's arms wrought.
While war in the far-off South
Mowed fields of death at the cannon's mouth;
His breath of fire and hail
Was not more dreadful than (that) the wail
Of want in the North, whose shiv'ring blast,
To mothers' hearts, and children's homes laid waste.

When the disconsolate East was blowing,
And not a spray nor leaf of cheer was flowing
With life's heavy stream;
And when the harsh skies hissing, snowing,
And low and dark and sullen growing,
Extinguished sun's last gleam.
When little bare foot want was going
From door to door;
Her withered empty hands a showing,
Her eyes running o'er—
Telling of a father dead,
Who for his country had bled;
And of a sick mother's bed,
Begging a crumb of bread;
When wretchedness her bare arms throwing
Around her children, looked thro' tears
And murmured in her country's ears

To help her in her sore distress
Feed those the war left fatherless;
When this hour came, the darkest hour
That e'er upon our flag did lower,
God called His man, as best He knows,
God called His man, and Morton rose.
Like some vast cliff whose tow'ring form
Awe, strikes but shelters from the storm,
He rose, to us a strong defense,
A tow'r of help, and good immense.

With Indiana on his back,
Her Legislature off the track,
And half the members pulling back,
He rose, the awful advocate,
And on the right road dragged his State.
Tho' wealth hugged his Secession gold,
And with a nod the weak controlled,
Things had to move when he took hold,
And shook to life the feeble souled.

Statesman, patriot, sire, bear him away;
Inter him with a nation's honors to-day!
He has seized slavery with fearless hands,
And thrown her gloomy castle from the sands,
His blows of massive wisdom strong,
Have hurled to earth the tow'ring wrong,
But 'neath its falling columns crushed,
His matchless voice in death is hushed.
Beauty, cover him with flowers of his native shore.
Valor, with unfading laurels cover him o'er.
Freedmen, bring your tears,
And till life's last years
Reach the echoless shore,
Tell his great deeds o'er.
And soldiers, wherever our standard flies;
Or where thou goest neath foreign skies,
Behold thy friend in death low lies!
Friend when you fronted the battle,

Friend when the cannon's rattle
Mowed a harvest of death,
Friend when "worn out" you reeled
Home from the bloody field
To rest beneath
An humble shed,
Scanty of comfort, scanty of bread—
Weep for him soldiers! Weep for your friend!
And forget not till your lives shall end,
To honor the noble dead.

Ye Bards of England

England, cannot thy shores boast bards as great,
And hearts as good as ever blest a State?
When arts were rude and literature was young,
And language faltered with an uncouth tongue;
When science trembled on her little hight,
And poor religion blundered on in night;
When song on Rome's vast tomb, or carved in Greek,
Like epitaphs with marble lips did speak,
Thy Chaucer singing with the Nightingales,
Poured forth his heart in Canterbury tales,
With rude shell scooped from English pure, and led
The age that raised the muses from the dead.

And gentle Thompson, to thy mem'ry dear,
Awake his lyre and sang the rolling year.
The dropping shower the wild flower scented mead,
The sober herds that in the noon shade feed,
The fragrant field, the green and shady wood,
The winding glen, and rocky solitude,
The smiles of Spring and frowns of Winter gray,
Alike employed his pure and gentle lay.
The wrath of gods, and armies dread suspense,
Celestial shouts and shock of arms immense,
In all his song ne'er move us to alarm,
But earth's pure sounds and sights allure and charm.

To Missolonghi's chief of singers too,
Unhappy Byron is a tribute due.
A wounded spirit, mournful and yet mad,
A genius proud, defiant, gentle, sad.
'Twas he whose Harold won his Nation's heart,
And whose Reviewers made her fair cheeks smart;
Whose uncurbed Juan hung her head for shame,
And whose Mazzeppa won unrivaled fame.
Earth had no bound for him. Where'er he strode
His restless genius found no fit abode.

The wing'd storm and the lightning tongued Jungfrau,
Unfathomable Ocean, and the awe
Of Alpine shades, the avalanche's groan,
The war-rocked empire and the falling throne,
Were toys his genius played with. Britain, then
Urn Byron's dust—a prodigy of men.
But Shakspeare, the inimitable boast
Of everybody and of every coast;
The *man*, whose universal fitness meets
Response in every heart of flesh that beats,
No tongue can tell him. One must feel his hand
And see him in his plays, to understand.
All thought to him intuitively's known,
The prate of clowns, and wisdoms of the throne,
The sophist's puzzles and the doctor's rules,
The skill of warriors and the cant of fools.
When Shakespeare wrote, the tragic muse saw heights,
Before nor since ne'er tempted in her flights.

THE GREAT STRIKE

"Strike! Strike! Stop! Stop!" What mean these shouts that rise—
This great commotion throughout all the land,
That chills the circling life of enterprise,
While lawlessness stalks forth with torch in hand?

The hands of Industry have to the head
(Aweary grown of swinging to and fro)
Without discretion's sober forethought said:
"We ought to be above, and you below."

Whenever Communism's snaky head
Is raised against the heel of Capital,
I want it crushed 'neath Law's majestic tread,
And yet would heed poor honest labor's call.

The cold long Winter fast is coming on,
His near approach makes sad the leafless year,
And deep snows soon the naked fields upon,
Will hush the voice of Autumn's latest cheer.

The burdened year will soon her treasures yield,
And pile our spacious barns from eaves to floor,
Then vagrant want in lanes and open field,
Can gather scanty sustenance no more.

The howling winds will drive before them then,
This drifting dust of Fortune's feet in clouds;
And hither thither into ditch and den
Mis'ry and crime will rush in babbling crowds.

But while the desp'rate curse, while lewdness cries,
And shiftlessness ought justly to go bare,
Forget it not, full many a Lazarus lies
Before thy gate and *needs* a crumb of care.

While Wealth across his lordly arm will cast
The warmth of scores of God Almighty's poor,

Still houseless want must shiver in the blast,
And childhood's feet go bare from door to door.

While pride upon her easy finger wears
The bread of thousands in a brilliant stone,
The eyes of Wretchedness must stream with tears,
And groaning labor be content to groan.

Let heaven's light upon our nature shine,
Till ev'ry opaque spot with glory beams,
And want no longer at our feet can pine,
But happiness will flow in living streams.

The Tramp's Soliloquy

Had I an envied name and purse of gold,
My friends were more than all my wants twice told;
Reduced to rags and born of title small,
Vast tho' my wants I have no friends at all.
Anxiety consumes away my years
And failure melts my manhood down in tears.
My down-cast eyes some guilt seem to disclose
And I'm shut in a lazar house of woes.
I am not what I was, my drooping form
Partakes of what is loathsome in the worm.
Pittied but not respected I *may* be,
I shun myself, and e'en the dogs shun me.
The rich to chide the poor may adulate
The few torn pleasures of a scanty state;
But cold experience tells her story plain,
Want breeds with bitterness and brings forth pain.

A Hint

Who seeks to show another's fault will find
In self a greater shown,
But he that is to faults of others blind,
But covers thus his own.

A.A. WHITMAN

A Note About the Author

A.A. Whitman (1851–1901) was an African American poet and minister. Born into slavery in Kentucky, Whitman was freed after the Emancipation Proclamation and worked for years as a laborer and teacher. He studied under Bishop Daniel Payne at Wilberforce University in 1870 before becoming a financial agent for the institution and a pastor in Springfield, Ohio. With his wife Caddie, he raised four daughters who eventually formed The Whitman Sisters, a famous vaudeville troupe that toured for over forty years beginning in 1900. In 1877, he published his debut collection *Not a Man, and Yet a Man*, which earned him a reputation as a leading African American poet in the tradition of Phillis Wheatley and Jupiter Hammon. Throughout his career, he published three collections of poems, including *An Idyl of the South: An Epic Poem in Two Parts* (1901), which appeared shortly before his death from pneumonia in 1901.

A Note from the Publisher

Spanning many genres, from non-fiction essays to literature classics to children's books and lyric poetry, Mint Edition books showcase the master works of our time in a modern new package. The text is freshly typeset, is clean and easy to read, and features a new note about the author in each volume. Many books also include exclusive new introductory material. Every book boasts a striking new cover, which makes it as appropriate for collecting as it is for gift giving. Mint Edition books are only printed when a reader orders them, so natural resources are not wasted. We're proud that our books are never manufactured in excess and exist only in the exact quantity they need to be read and enjoyed. To learn more and view our library, go to minteditionbooks.com

bookfinity & MINT EDITIONS

Enjoy more of your favorite classics with Bookfinity,
a new search and discovery experience for readers.
With Bookfinity, you can discover more vintage
literature for your collection, find your Reader Type,
track books you've read or want to read,
and add reviews to your favorite books.
Visit www.bookfinity.com, and click on
Take the Quiz to get started.

Don't forget to follow us
@bookfinityofficial and @mint_editions

9 781513 282619